Free Will Revisited

Free Will Revisited

A Respectful Response to Luther, Calvin, and Edwards

Robert E. Picirilli

WIPF & STOCK · Eugene, Oregon

FREE WILL REVISITED
A Respectful Response to Luther, Calvin, and Edwards

Wipf & Stock
An Imprint of Wipf and Stock Publishers
199 W. 8th Ave., Suite 3
Eugene, OR 97401

www.wipfandstock.com

PAPERBACK ISBN: 978-1-5326-1846-8
HARDCOVER ISBN: 978-1-4982-4404-6
EBOOK ISBN: 978-1-4982-4403-9

Manufactured in the U.S.A.   MAY 3, 2017

Quotations from John Calvin are from *The Bondage and Liberation of the Will: A Defence of the Orthodox Doctrine of Human Choice against Pighius.* Edited by A. N. S. Lane, translated by G. I. Davies. Grand Rapids: Baker, 1996. Used by permission.

Quotations from Martin Luther are from *Martin Luther on the Bondage of the Will: A New Translation of* De Servo Arbitrio *(1525), Martin Luther's Reply to Erasmus of Rotterdam.* Translated by J. I. Packer and O. R. Johnston. Westwood, NJ: Revell, 1957. Used by permission of James Clarke and Co. (UK).

Quotations from Jonathan Edwards are from *Freedom of the Will.* Edited by Paul Ramsey. The Works of Jonathan Edwards 1. New Haven, CT: Yale University Press, 1957.

Scripture quotations, unless otherwise indicated, are from the New King James Version, copyright © 1982 by Thomas Nelson. Used by permission. All rights reserved.

Contents

Preface

IT IS HARD TO disagree with people who wear halos. And Luther, Calvin, and Edwards—each one a giant—deserve theirs. I would be the last to question the honored place they have in the history of the Christian church and its thinkers.

Some readers may therefore question my sanity in taking them on. I certainly do not do so lightly. But I know from long experience that our heroes, like ourselves, are sometimes wrong in one belief or another, and I think that these men, and others who follow them in this matter, are wrong in denying the freedom of the human will. Their denial may result, in part, from misunderstanding that concept or its implications.

They denied free will, I think, because they were contending for the faith once delivered to the saints when it was threatened by a theology that regarded humanity too highly. This was especially true of Luther and Calvin, who after all carried the burden of freeing us from bondage to a corrupt Roman church with its wrongheaded doctrine of humanity and salvation. This was to some degree true for Edwards also, who was aware of similar tendencies in the Church of England of his day. Neither of the three men dealt with that wing of Reformed theology represented by the early forerunners of Baptist orthodoxy, like the Anabaptists and early English General Baptists. Nor did they deal with the writings of Jacobus Arminius, the Dutch theologian who more than any other one person influenced this thinking. They were likewise unacquainted with the sounder treatments of the more evangelical Arminians, like Wesley and those under his influence.

To say that is not to criticize. Luther and Calvin could not have read Arminius or the English General Baptists or Wesley. The two Reformers preceded all the theologians who represent the Arminian wing of Reformed theology, except for the scattered and still-developing Anabaptists. Edwards apparently did not have Arminius available to him, and the only "Arminians" he read were tainted with questionable and inconsistent theological influences in the Church of England and the religious milieu of the time.

Consequently, the concept of free will resisted by the three men whose books against free will I will interact with included elements that did not represent sound, biblical theology. For that matter, Arminianism has not always represented such a sound and consistent view of things. My purpose, therefore, includes setting the doctrine of free will in its proper, biblical context, and this will include giving due consideration to such matters as the sovereignty and providence of God, the total depravity of human nature after the fall, and salvation by grace alone through faith alone.

Before undertaking this work, I determined on a specific approach: namely, to deal with the subject as it was argued, specifically, by Luther, Calvin, and Edwards. I picked them because each of these theological masters wrote a volume against free will, and because these are perhaps the best known and most influential books to make a case against free will. The three men are highly regarded, and rightly so. (Even to say that is an understatement.) I have not dealt with the other works of these men, confidently assuming that whatever they had to say about free will is to be found in the books they devoted to that very subject.

I have also chosen not to treat, in detail, the other doctrines of the Calvinistic wing of Reformed theology except as they bear directly on the question of free will. The reason for this is that I have already published most of what I care to say on those doctrines. My volume entitled *Grace, Faith, Free Will* is everywhere assumed in this work and can be consulted for much more thorough treatment of any part of the theology of salvation. In that volume, however, I did not defend the *concept* of free will. This volume will both define and defend the concept and should therefore serve as something of a companion volume to my earlier one.

The reader will probably also note that, except for extensive citing of Luther's, Calvin's, and Edwards's volumes against free will, I have not interacted with or cited much from other authors. One reason for this is that I have already done this sort of thing with the soteriological issues involved in my earlier work and do not feel the need to cover that ground again. Another reason—the main one no doubt—is that I intended this book to represent specifically my own personal interaction with Luther, Calvin, and Edwards, and only on the subject of free will and its direct implications.

A biblical concept of free will is important for many reasons. It does not exalt humanity too highly; no more highly than God himself lifted them in creating them to bear his own image. Nor does it demean humankind too much; no more than humanity demeaned itself in wicked disobedience against God, and so in bearing the consequences of that rebellion in a wholly corrupted and sinful nature that leaves them dead and deaf to spiritual truth, blind, and bound in sin.

Is it possible that such beings have a will that is free to make choices between alternative courses of action? To answer this is the purpose of this work.

Abbreviations

Citations from Luther, Calvin, and Edwards

BECAUSE THERE WILL BE many citations from the following three volumes, I have chosen to avoid the multiplication of footnotes that would result, instead citing them in parentheses using these abbreviations, with page numbers.

BW   Martin Luther, *Martin Luther on the Bondage of the Will: A New Translation of* De Servo Arbitrio *(1525), Martin Luther's Reply to Erasmus of Rotterdam*, translated by J. I. Packer and O. R. Johnston (Westwood, NJ: Revell, 1957)

BLW   John Calvin, *The Bondage and Liberation of the Will: A Defence of the Orthodox Doctrine of Human Choice against Pighius*, edited by A. N. S. Lane, translated by G. I. Davies (Grand Rapids: Baker, 1996)

FW   Jonathan Edwards, *Freedom of the Will*, edited by Paul Ramsey (Works of Jonathan Edwards 1; New Haven, CT: Yale University Press, 1957)

Part One

Defining the Issues

1

What Is Free Will?

THE FIRST STEP IN the serious discussion of any issue ought to be a clear definition of the issue. I begin, therefore, by explaining what I mean by the freedom of the will.

Free will is not a "thing," not a distinct substance or essence that makes up one part of a human being. To say that a person *has* free will is not the same as saying that a person *has* a body—or a spirit or soul. (I have no interest, here, in the debate whether humans are two- or three-part beings.)

What is clear is that a person has—or *is?*—a *will*. I assume that the reader—any Christian reader, at least—will agree. The noun *will* is closely associated with, and its meaning is involved with, other words like *desire, purpose, intention, determination*, and *decision*. To say that a person has a will is to say that a person experiences purpose, intends things, and makes decisions. Machines do not do that sort of thing, regardless how sophisticated they are. We only anthropomorphize when we say something like, "My computer thinks I want the next word after a period to be capitalized." Computers, as marvelous as they are, do not "think" at all; they only do what they are programmed to do by people who do think. They do not make decisions; they experience no purposes achieved or thwarted. Only human beings, only essences that are conscious of themselves as selves, function in such ways. Only such an essence can *will*. (*Will* works at least as well as a verb as a noun.)

To describe the human will as *free* is to say something about the way it functions. In one sense, then, to speak of the will as free is to say something redundant. Be careful how you deny free will: you may very well deny the will itself. To be sure, when we use the term *free will* we intend to convey the notion that *choices* are involved. But that notion is already inherent in the unmodified word. The first definition my dictionary gives for *will* is, "the power of making a reasoned choice or decision."[1] To say that persons exercise their wills is little if anything more than to say that they choose. Any such choice or decision we call a *volition*, an act or exercise of the will.

At least one of the three giants whose writings against free will I will interact with in this volume would seem to agree with what I have just said. Jonathan Edwards defines the will—not *free* will, as such—as "that by which the mind chooses anything," a "faculty or power or principle of mind by which it is capable of choosing," "an act of the will is the same as an act of choosing" (*FW* 137). As I will show later, he goes on to say that a will can choose without being free. I am more inclined to think that if there is no freedom then there is no choosing, so that a will, by definition, is free.

I am not pretending that the matter is that simple, but I am saying that this ought to be the starting point for exploring the issue. Before we argue about depravity, about whether fallen human beings still possess free wills—or *wills* at all—we had better say clearly what we mean to affirm or deny in the discussion of free will. And I offer, now, a basic definition of free will that I think we can use as a starting point for further discussion:

Free Will is a way of saying that a person is capable of making decisions, that a person can choose between two (or more) alternatives when he or she has obtained (by whatever means) the degree of understanding of those alternatives required to choose between them.

I intend for this definition to involve what is traditionally stated as "the power of alternative choice," also sometimes called "libertarian freedom." This means that the choice or decision is one that really could go either way; that the person is neither compelled by some force outside nor shut up from within by previous condition or experience, so that only one alternative can actually be chosen. In other words, possessing a free will—or a will, for that matter, as I would contend—rules out determinism and compatibilism. I will say more about these in the next chapter. For now, it is enough to say that both of these are forms of determinism, given that compatibilism by definition includes the idea that determinism and freedom are compatible. Another name for compatibilism is "soft determinism," after all. My definition, then, is intentionally set against all forms of determinism and in support of *self-determinism*. It is the very nature of a *self* to exercise will.

---

1. *Webster's New World College Dictionary*, 1528.

I also intend my definition to allow that making choices requires some level of understanding as to what the choices are. This means more than one thing. One is that the choices we call *free* are not merely random but are rational or reasoned. There is no *will* apart from the *mind* of a *self*. The will is perhaps an aspect or attribute of a mind—but I do not intend, here, a technical description of personhood. Nor do I intend to qualify a real choice as requiring understanding of everything involved in the choice, like all the reasons for and against it or all the consequences. But the one who chooses between two (or more) alternatives must at least perceive what those choices are and that he can choose between them.

I also intend my definition, without avoiding the implications of depravity, to make a distinction between the capacity of the will and the circumstances within which the will is able to operate freely. First we define free will and *then* we can talk about how depravity affects it and where grace must intervene. Each of those issues can be defined in its own right and confusion can be avoided.

When I say this I am reflecting on the fact that the Calvinistic wing of Reformed theology denies that fallen humanity possesses free will, at least if free will means the ability to choose between alternatives. I would suggest that many people—to some degree with justification—take this to mean the same thing as a naturalistic mechanism or fatalism. It matters little to people whether "determinism" is a result of the blind cause-effect laws of a purposeless cosmos or of the deliberate intention of an all-controlling God. Determinism from either source makes no allowance for human freedom, since human choices determine nothing.

I regard it as obvious that the ability of a person to *will* is part of what it means to bear the image of God, and that fallen humanity still bears that image, as 1 Corinthians 11:7 indicates. I offer, then, that the freedom of the human will is *constitutional*. One's will is always "there" as an aspect of human nature, a way persons *function*. Depravity does not change the fact that a person has a will or that it is constitutionally *free* to make choices. To be sure, the circumstances in which the will functions bear on whether the person can choose this or that alternative, and that is where depravity gets involved. A person in prison, for example, has not lost the capacity to walk the streets unchained, but his circumstances curtail his ability to exercise that capacity at the time.

Just so, depravity limits our choices without our losing the constitutional capacity to choose. How, then, can a fallen person ever be "free" to choose for God? I will deal with this more fully in a later chapter on free will, depravity, and grace. For now, it is enough to say—and this is the point of the latter part of my definition, above—that such a person must obtain a level of understanding of the choices available.

To some degree, although not as fully as I think is required, Calvin and Luther (less so) acknowledged the existence of this constitutional capacity. Luther spoke of it as a "dispositional quality," but he was willing to name it "free will" only in respect to what is "below" human beings and not to what is "above" them, only in the realm of nature and not in the realm of grace (*BW* 105, 265). Calvin made some distinction between what it means to will *as such* and to will *for good or ill*. The first he called "the faculty of willing" and the second "qualities of opposed habits." Of the first he said it is "perpetually resident in our nature," but he urged that its evil condition at present represents a corruption of nature that finally belongs to the power itself (*BLW* 209). He went on to say that in regeneration a new substance is not implanted, but that this change affects "habit" (*BLW* 210).

All three of the men I am interacting with, however, back away from this constitutional capacity when they discuss the will of fallen humanity. They are so dominated by thoughts of the effects of the fall and the helplessness of fallen persons that in effect—and in words, for that matter—they deny that humanity any longer possesses free will. And, given what it means to be able to will, this seems to be no better than to deny that fallen persons have a will at all.

To believe in the freedom of the will as I have defined it above, then, applies to choices of any sort. They include everyday decisions that seem entirely innocent and unimportant, like which socks to wear today (almost, but not quite, inconsequential) or which restaurant to take your wife to for your anniversary celebration (very consequential!). They include much more important moral choices: whether to lie to avoid a predicament, or whether to retaliate when wronged. And they include the ultimate choice that leads to eternal life: putting faith in Jesus Christ. But in all of these, there must at least be some understanding of what the choices are for there to be freedom of choice in the circumstances.

Free Will as Self-Determinism

If I have consciously defined free will in a way that is opposed to all forms of determinism, including soft determinism (compatibilism), I may add that it is also not the same as *indeterminism*. Generally speaking, indeterminism is the view that there are at least some events in the universe that have no cause at all and arise spontaneously. In such usage "spontaneously" is difficult to define: it may mean nothing more than randomly or accidentally or in a way that cannot be explained.

At the extreme, indeterminism might say that *nothing* can be explained in terms of cause and effect, and in that case one would wonder why the cosmos is orderly rather than in utter chaos. Such a radical indeterminism would be rare, indeed. People who call themselves indeterminists will more likely say that there are *some* events in the universe that occur without being caused, especially some of the actions of persons. Human volitions, by this view, are often free and "undetermined."

For this view, however, *self-determinism* is a better term than *indeterminism*. The things selves do, including the choices or decisions that are the grounds for their actions, are not undetermined but are determined within themselves. If one prefers the language of cause and effect, then one may say that persons cause their own actions, or at least that the causes are not other entities outside themselves. But the language of cause and effect is not the best way to describe the functions of the mind or will of persons. Physical events can be explained by cause-effect laws that determine them or make them necessary, but personal events are often of a different nature and cannot always be explained in that way. Thoughts and decisions can arise in the mind without being determined by entities outside ourselves.

As we will see in the chapter on Edwards, he objected strongly to this and ridiculed the idea of self-determinism. I will deal with the matter more thoroughly in the chapter on free will and the rationalism of Edwards. It seems enough to observe, here, that the concept of free will, as I have defined it, implies self-determinism, and that this in turn means that much (not all) of human behavior involves contingencies rather than necessities. To speak of contingencies is to speak of things that might be or not be, of things that really might be one way or another—the power of alternative choice, in other words. Necessities are things that can be only the way they are. I will return to this in the chapter on free will, foreknowledge, and necessity.

2

Free Will and the Clash of Worldviews

THE CONCEPT OF FREE will, as defined in the previous chapter, stands in contrast to a number of different worldviews. I include here some discussion about the two of these that are most important for my present purposes.

Naturalistic Determinism

Twenty-first-century Western culture is dominated, intellectually and practically, by the mindset of secular science. Not even the popularity of postmodern subjectivism, in my opinion, has changed that.

One would be foolish to deny the power of science, gained by its myriad achievements. It has proved itself right so often that anyone who questions that it has everything right seems sure to be a fool in the end. Consider the successes of science and bend the knee in awe and submission; that seems the wiser course.

Those successes are legendary and legion. When I was a youngster, for example, every summer brought a new wave of fear that some of us would come down with polio. Our president in his wheelchair was a living reminder of its debilitating effects. But who now is afraid of "infantile paralysis"—or of the big, bad wolf? Science conquered poliomyelitis—and a hundred other diseases and superstitions.

Not long ago, as time should be measured, our scientists actually rocketed human beings into space, and into orbit around the moon. Some of them descended to and walked on the surface of the moon. More astounding, they ascended back to the main ship and broke free of the moon's gravity and returned to earth, safe and sound. That was a stunning achievement, and people practicing science exulted in what they did—and well they should. (And already, unbelievably, we take it for granted.)

Just during my lifetime, in technology alone, we have become jaded with the new toys that effectively reroute our lives. I remember well attending the World's Fair in New York in 1940 and being mesmerized by the vision of the future that was showcased there. Science has far exceeded that projection. Who knew that Dick Tracy's wristwatch radio was anything more than a whimsy of imagination?

I see no need to multiply illustrations, as easy as that would be. My point is simply this: science has clearly earned its reputation and its hold on our thinking. Who can possibly question the efficacy of its method?

Science is, of course, a method, one with a name: the *empirical method*. To oversimplify, this method, at root, touts the gaining of knowledge by experience. The experience meant is sense experience, what comes to us by sight, hearing, touch, taste, and smell. Expressing this a little more fully, the method works this way: Gather all the facts of experience possible, then propose a theory or hypothesis that would explain all those facts. Proceed, next, to test the hypothesis by examining yet more experience, especially by setting up experiences (experiments) that can falsify or verify the hypothesis. If the hypothesis needs adjusting to fit new facts of experience, do so. And continue this process indefinitely until the hypothesis has been suitably refined and tested in every conceivable way and shown to give consistent results. Along the way, one gains more and more confidence in the hypothesis, ultimately coming to trust it as truth. Even so, one knows that this "truth" may yet be shown false or inadequate by some experiences not now anticipated.

Do not ridicule that method. It is the basis for the conquest of polio and the moon. It works. *It is the right method for matters of science.* Were I in the practice of some branch of science, it is the method I would use. And in various ways all of us are in the practice of science from time to time.

Something else needs to be said, however. Science, as most professionals do science, and as it is perceived by the great majority of us who observe and benefit from it, is *more* than a method. It is also an affirmation about other paths to knowledge. In short, secular science insists that its method—empiricism—is the *only* way to knowledge. Such an affirmation has numerous implications, of course. One is that no other method—neither rationalism nor revelation, for example—can lead us to knowledge and so to truth.

Closely related, this affirmation means that all truth, all knowledge in which we put confidence, must be confined to the sphere in which the scientific method works. That sphere, as the method indicates by definition, is the sphere of sense experience. According to secular science, then, one can know only the world of the senses, only the physical world. There is, in fact, no other world.

The meaning of this is clear. There is no truth except empirical truth, the truth yielded by the practice of the scientific method. It is not possible to know anything at all about any reality that is not "physical." There can be no truth about any so-called spiritual realm or God. There is no such realm, and if there is it can't be known, because we have nothing but the scientific method by which to apprehend reality.

What seems to have escaped notice is an internal contradiction in this affirmation about the scientific method. The claim that nothing can be known except by the scientific method—or, to put it positively, that we can know truth only by empirical method—is clearly a claim to state truth. And yet this truth claim *is itself not arrived at or known by the empirical/ scientific method!* This simple fact puts the lie to the claim. One can claim, "I know this or that by empirical method." But one manifestly cannot claim, "There is no other way to know anything" except as an expression of blind, unsupported faith.

This fatal flaw does not, however, keep the secular scientists from many more confident affirmations, all growing out of their use of the scientific method complemented by faith that there is no other way to knowledge and so no other truth. As a result, the secular scientific enterprise, intoxicated by its breathtaking successes in the realms where the method works, goes on to fashion a worldview that the academic elite confidently indoctrinate into the culture at large via the educational system and the media. And, impressed by science's successes—not to mention their own desire to be their own gods— far too many swallow the line they spoon-feed us.

For that reason, then, there is no beauty; there is only "conditioning." We are conditioned to think that there is objective beauty in the flowers or in a skillful artist's landscape. This is a habit we have developed, largely as a result of the influence of others who developed the habit before us. But when reality is analyzed in accord with atomic theory, an alley in a slum, with garbage piled on both sides, is no less beautiful than a sunset over the Pacific. *Beautiful* is just a word we use to describe certain physical sensations that we've been conditioned to experience in certain ways.

Likewise, there is no meaning or purpose; there is only sensual desire, frustrated or satisfied. In the secular worldview saturating our culture, there is no reason that anything exists. Words like *reason, meaning,* and *purpose* are appropriate only for a world where there are personal beings who can think and choose. But in a world where every organism is, alike, nothing more than protoplasm and neural circuits, all of them are equally and entirely physical, differing only in the adaptive abilities that have evolved over the course of eons. None of them came into existence for any reason, and none of them—human beings included—are headed for any realization of cosmic purpose. The existentialists are right: our existence means nothing except for the subjective "meaning" we can infuse into it for a moment, and then we vanish into nothingness. Life is absurd.

Furthermore, there are no minds; there are only bodies. The so-called mind is nothing more than a fanciful "ghost in the machine," a name we give to certain complexities of brain activity. Dissect a body as much as you wish; you will find nothing "there" except for the matter or energy that is expressed in the circuits that transmit sense-based impulses and "wire" our bodies together to react to various physical stimuli.

Then there are no moral absolutes; there is only relativity and subjectivity. In a world without God there is no ultimate standard for right and wrong. To be sure, societies devise rules that are pragmatic and promote "the common good," as defined in a particular culture. But there are no universals, and this applies to morality before everything else.

And so, at last, there is no freedom; there is only mechanism. All physical things—and all things are physical—are essentially the same kind of stuff, functioning according to the laws of nature. There is no supernatural realm, nothing real that is not part of *nature*. The laws of nature function, essentially, according to cause-and-effect relationships. Each event is the effect of a prior cause that is, in turn, the effect of a prior cause. Nothing that occurs is free, regardless of how it seems, but is as predictable as the law of gravity. True, some human behavior seems more complex than this, but when it is carefully analyzed one can see that the choices made by human beings are not free but are the certain results of prior states that produced them. We are computers—very sophisticated ones, of course—and all our actions are "programmed" by a programmer that isn't there! Freedom is an illusion, yet another habit of behavior.

And so the view of secular science is a *worldview.* A worldview is a construct that one hopes will make sense of everything in experience—and not just his or her personal experience but the experience of everyone on the globe. This particular worldview tends to dominate the thinking of Western culture in our day. It is, at root, naturalistic or materialistic or physicalistic, contending that there is no supernatural or spiritual reality, only nature and physical bodies. It is mechanistic, contending that all events, including apparently free choices, derive from complex causal relationships. It is pessimistic, contending that there is no ultimate good or purpose, no meaning for existence. It is pragmatic and utilitarian, contending that ideas about beauty and morality are only true insofar as they are useful, and that is what *true* means.

I have taken the time to describe the worldview of secular science, even though in summary fashion, in order to make recognizable the true enemy of freedom of the will. Anyone who discounts this freedom needs to understand the worldview that provides a grounds for doing so. Without striving too hard for philosophical precision, let's call it *naturalism*. As an all-encompassing worldview, naturalism has no room within it for free choices, whether in matters small or large, of little consequence or determining the destiny of the human race.

We *think* we make free choices, of course. Only the most sophisticated scientists and philosophers doubt that—and one suspects that even they think *they* make free choices. At the simplest level, a person dresses for the day and assumes she freely chooses which of her many outfits she will wear that day. Not really, say the mechanists: were she aware of all the subtle influences that affect her decision, past and present, she might just realize that her choice was already determined and that all the electrical impulses crossing the synapses in her brain left her free to make no other choice but the one she made.

Apply this to matters of serious consequence like moral choices. Just as certainly, a certain criminal commits murder as a result of a cause-and-effect chain that began long before he can remember. None of his decisions were really free. And so with religion: as a machine, a human being is not able to make truly free choices about gods and destiny.

The freedom of the will is, by contrast to all this, grounded in a *Christian* worldview. In this worldview there is a personal God who has inaugurated space and time outside himself, into which he has created a physical universe that includes human beings that are personal—like their Creator in significant ways. As persons they are rational and moral beings, though fallen into sin and depravity. They are capable of grasping beauty, of sensing meaning, of discerning purpose in things, including in their own existence. In turn, they are able to purpose things, to make choices that they (correctly or mistakenly) believe will contribute to the achievement of their purposes. In distinctively Christian terms, they have freedom of choice as a constitutional endowment, though it has been severely affected by their spiritual condition apart from God.

This is not the place to explain such matters in detail; that will come later in this volume. For now, however, it is important to say that freedom of will, the power of choice between live alternative possibilities, is part of a world where people are more than physical bodies, where meaning and purpose for existence are actively at work, where there is objective beauty that may be perceived and understood, where moral responsibility cannot be shunned, where the spirit and mind are as real as the body, and where, finally, one chooses between heaven and hell.

Be careful, then, how you give up freedom of will. You may give up beauty, meaning, purpose, and personhood with it. You may, in fact, concede dominance to what is at root an impersonal, deterministic naturalism.

I would submit that in order to give full glory to God as Creator of the cosmos and of persons in his image, you will need to save some place for freedom of will in your account of human nature. Let it be as negatively affected as you wish, or as you believe the Bible requires—and we will pursue this in other chapters—there needs to be such freedom as a part of the constitution of human beings in a Christian worldview.

Theological Determinism

Not all forms of determinism are expressions of naturalism. The concept of free will—again, the previous chapter has defined this—stands in contrast to *all* forms of determinism, including those espoused by theologians. And theologians *do* espouse determinism in various forms.

Without getting too specific, I will define theological determinism as the view that everything that happens in the universe, including the apparently free choices of human beings, comes about as a result of the fact that God, before the foundation of the world, deliberately decreed everything that will transpire as part of his all-inclusive plan.

Of course, this definition is capable of being interpreted in more than one way, given that it is dependent on *words*, and the meanings of words are somewhat negotiable. Even so, according to theological determinism, a person's choices (1) can be only the way they are and (2) are directly or indirectly determined by God. It will become clear in subsequent chapters that all three of the advocates against free will whom I have chosen to inter-act with in this volume—Luther, Calvin, and Edwards—were determinists.

Theological determinists do not deny that human beings make choices; they simply affirm that their choices are the only ones they are capable of making. And this introduces a major issue in determinism of any stripe: if a person is free to make only one choice, is that a *free* choice? Indeed, is it really a *choice*, after all? It is a *volition*, of course, taking this word to mean an exercise of the will, a decision to act. Is it, however, the activity of a *free will*? The previous chapter has defined free will to include the power of alternative choice, also referred to as "libertarian freedom." (As though *freedom* needs another word meaning the same thing to qualify it!) Perhaps most people, if asked to say what free will means, would include the idea that the person is free to choose between two or more alternative courses of action.

The views of John Calvin, and of those who follow his main theologi-cal conclusions (especially in regard to the theology of salvation), we call *Calvinism*. Calvinism—no doubt including Luther and Edwards—typically defends determinism in a form called *soft determinism*. Another name for this is *compatibilism*. (Neither term was in use when Luther and Calvin wrote against free will; compatibilism was not when Edwards wrote.)

Soft determinism, or compatibilism, holds that determinism (as de-fined above) and human freedom are compatible. In other words, one can believe, without being incoherent, both that God determines all things and yet that humans act freely and not by constraint. But this does not say *how* the two apparently contradictory ideas are compatible, so we need additional definition. Soft determinism holds that persons always act "freely" but, at the same time, always in the one way that is determined by the sum total of their understanding, desires, intentions, and purposes at the time they act.

For the sake of brevity, we may sum up all these words in one: *motiva-tion*. In compatibilism, persons are free to act in accord with their motiva-tion, but motivation is of such a nature as to allow for just one course of action. And this is true for relatively insignificant matters, like the brand of toothpaste one purchases, and for matters of the highest significance, like moral decisions.

We may illustrate with a girl tempted to steal a banana from the grocer's display. No one is looking and she faces a choice: pick it up, put it in her coat pocket, and leave; or resist the temptation. What will "determine" the choice? The compatibilist says that it will be determined by the person's motivation, by the sum total of everything in her experience that has any influence on her at the time. Is she hungry? What was she taught by her parents or others who influenced her thinking? Has she stolen before, without being caught, and found it thrilling to steal? Add in everything else that contributes to her state of mind, consciously or unconsciously, and only one choice is possible. It is a choice that is made necessary—that is, *caused*—by everything leading up to it, the only one she can actually make; yet it is a "free" choice, since the girl is not coerced and decides without constraint.

None of us would deny that sometimes our choices are this way. Given everything that contributes to who we are and how we think at a particular time (some of which we may not be aware of), only one choice may be possible. Nor would we deny that sometimes even our moral choices are limited because of prior choices. We really can, by wrong choices, get ourselves in a set of circumstances, at times, when no right choice is even available. And we would not argue against being held accountable in such instances. If a prior bad choice made it so that a present choice must be bad, we are guilty on both counts.

But is this true for *all* the choices we make? For various reasons our instinct is to say no, that we are not *always* limited by who and what we are so that *every* choice can be only the one we make. The most important reason for our saying this is found in our own experience. In our choosing we *experience* things that seem clearly to contradict the compatibilist notion that only one choice is possible. We experience the pull of two different possibilities. We experience debating within ourselves the pros and cons of both options. We experience strong desires both ways. Sometimes, in indecision, we decide to "flip a coin" and go with it. Sometimes we experience choosing against what we'd rather do, against our own desires, for one reason or another. Sometimes we choose the way we prefer in spite of knowing that it is wrong. *We almost always, in such battles, experience going with one choice while being certain that we could have made the other choice.* Again, this applies both to matters of indifference and to important things, things with eternal consequences.

In such instances as these, we experience and believe in human freedom. Not *absolute* freedom, of course. Only God is absolutely free. But freedom, nonetheless, and freedom to choose between alternatives, to choose in more than one way.

To all of this the compatibilists reply that, yes, they understand our experience. They have had similar experiences. But regardless how much we *think* we could have made the other choice, we really did not have that freedom. If we just understood the weight of all the factors that affected our thoughts and feelings at the time (our motivation), we would realize that only one choice was possible: namely, the choice we made. Indeed, some of the contributing factors we were not even conscious of.

In making such an argument as this, the compatibilist has retreated into what we may call an *unfalsifiable* position. This means that no matter what experience or argument we may insist on, the answer will be, "It *seems* that way, but you just aren't aware of all that's affecting you. You only *think* you could have made the other choice, but you really couldn't. You must act in accord with your own desire, even when you think your desire is different from the way you decide." There is then no way to show that the compatibilists' response is false, because they always know more than we do, always know better than the way we experience things.

I am not saying, by the way, that retreating into an unfalsifiable position necessarily makes a person wrong. All of us do that, at times, when we are faced with things that we cannot explain in terms of our worldview— things that, even so, do not change our minds. But when one reaches this point, he needs to understand that he is not making a further argument for his view and is not being persuasive. He is merely reasserting his position in the face of another's testimony.

In theological discussion of the issue we cannot avoid the problem of original sin and depravity, matters that will be discussed again in a subsequent chapter. For now, I will observe that our ability to make moral choices has clearly been affected, negatively, by the corruption of our nature stemming from the first sin by our progenitor, Adam. We are in a condition where our motivation, by nature, is to sin and our understanding has been so darkened that the judgments we make will lead us astray. (As I noted in the previous chapter, this does not mean we have lost the capacity to choose between alternatives; it only means that we are in circumstances that do not allow us to exercise that freedom with discernment.)

Even so, our situation results from free choice. Given that we sinned in Adam (Romans 5:12), the situation is precisely one where our "first" choice made it so that our freedom is restricted. Still, if we are identified with Adam in that sin, then we are identified with him in the *free* choice he made at the time. And in that case we still face the question of whether he (and we) could have made the alternative choice. We who affirm free will are confident that he could. As we will see in the chapter on Calvin, even he affirmed that Adam, as created, exercised free will in committing sin. And if we sinned with him, we also exercised free will in that.

The issue, then, is whether soft determinism offers *freedom* at all. Ever since this view was promulgated in modern times by philosophers like David Hume and Thomas Hobbes, other philosophers have responded with sharp criticism at this very point. Indeed, the term "soft determinism" was apparently invented by the pragmatist William James as something of a mockery of the compatibilist view, which he called a "quagmire of evasion" and said it involved stealing the word *freedom* to hide the determinism beneath it.[1] Immanuel Kant, similarly, called it a "wretched subterfuge" and "word jugglery" for misusing the word *free*.[2]

For my purposes, however, I am content to say that this view of free will is *not* what the defenders of free will uphold. It is not the power of alternative choice. It does not provide for libertarian freedom. And we are confident that real free will upholds these things and is in better accord with human experience and the teaching of the Scriptures. It is the purpose of the rest of this book to set forth this concept on biblical and theological grounds. As indicated in the previous chapter, the proper alternative to determinism, whether naturalistic or theological, is self-determinism.

---

1. James, *Will to Believe*, 149.

2. Kant, *Critique of Practical Reason*, 332.

3

Free Will in a Biblical Perspective

ALL CHRISTIANS SHOULD AGREE that what matters most, in the discussion of free will (or any theological issue), is what the Bible says. No amount of philosophical—or even "systematic theological"—argument can be as important, or determinative, as what is revealed in Holy Scripture.

The problem is that the Bible never undertakes to speak directly to the issue of whether people have the capacity for freedom of choice. To raise or settle that question is not part of the biblical agenda. Most so-called biblical answers to the question, then, are answers derived from putting together the implications of other biblically clear truths. These are usually "logical" constructs.

Here is an example of this sort of construct. The Bible teaches that salvation is wholly the work of God, and that humanity can make no contribution to that. To exercise free choice between receiving Christ and rejecting him would be such a contribution. Therefore, human beings can have no such freedom of choice.

Here is another example, on the opposite side of the issue. The Bible teaches that Jesus died for all, that all are invited to receive Christ and be saved, and that those who are lost are responsible for that. For humans to be held responsible for the rejection of Christ, they must have the freedom to choose or reject his provision for them. Therefore, humanity has freedom of choice.

Most of us can recognize the logical assumptions and reasoning involved in such arguments as these, and I will not deal with them here. Some of them will be important matters of discussion in subsequent parts of this book. But such discussions, as significant as they may be, do not really focus on how the Bible treats freedom of will as such.

Does the Bible, then, uphold freedom of will? If so, how? The answer, it seems to me, is that the Bible *everywhere assumes*, in its presentation of the interaction between God and humans, freedom of will. The whole Bible, in other words, depicts for us the history of free will—as a matter of responding in faith to the gracious offer of God, versus choosing instead to live in dark, eternal separation from him.

We most certainly need to take the Bible *as a whole*. It is all too easy to look at this text or that text and say that God is a sovereign being who is in control of everything, or to say that salvation is entirely his work, or to say that human beings are miserable worms and all credit and glory for salvation must go to God. *All of those things are true*, rightly understood. And there are texts to back up each one.

> Psalm 115:3 says, "Our God is in heaven: He does whatever He pleases."
>
> Romans 9:18 says, "He has mercy on whom He wills, and whom He wills He hardens."

Yes and yes. God saves only those whom he wills to save, and he saves them by grace without their contributing anything. But in order to see those truths as they relate to all other truths, we must go beyond the proof texts and read the Bible through. It depicts the playing out of a cosmic drama. "All the world's a stage," Shakespeare said—and the Bible is the script. We must look at the characters, at what they say to one another. We need to read it for motif and meaning. When we do, I'm convinced that what we find there is a history of free will and its challenges.

There is not space here for the whole Bible, of course, but a few of the highlights will reveal the whole.

The First Sin

Start with Adam and Eve in the garden (where else would one start?) in Genesis 2:16–17:

> *And the Lord God commanded the man, saying, "Of every tree of the garden you may freely eat: but of the tree of the knowledge of good and evil you shall not eat, for in the day that you eat of it you shall surely die."*

This certainly sounds like freedom of choice.

I hear someone cry "Foul!" And I understand. "That was *before* the fall, before humanity was depraved," says the one who objects to free will. "Yes, Adam had freedom of will then, but when he fell into sin that freedom was lost. Since then, freedom of the will is a myth."

I will accept that the experience of our original parents does not serve to settle the question of free will beyond Eden. Even so, I need to make a few observations about free will before the fall. One reason is that Edwards, at least, says enough to raise questions about the freedom of Adam and Eve before their sin. He observes that God, when he created humankind, so ordered "his 'circumstances, that from these circumstances, together with his [God's] withholding further assistance and divine influence, his sin would infallibly follow" (*FW* 413). In sustaining this, Edwards distinguishes between God's *perceptive* and his *disposing* will. The first expresses what God loves, as in his counsels and invitations, and presumably includes the instructions to Adam and Eve. The second expresses "what he chooses as a part of his own infinite scheme of things" (*FW* 415), which presumably includes their sin. While these statements are open to some interpretation, at the least Edwards means that God placed Adam in a set of circumstances where his sin was the only and necessary choice. That is not the circumstance of free will as I have defined it.

If Luther discussed the free will of Adam and Eve before the fall, I missed it. Calvin, however, clearly affirmed that Adam and Eve possessed free will before the fall. He says that humanity as created was "endowed . . . with sound intelligence of mind and uprightness of will." Furthermore, our present state of bondage to sin came about as a result of Adam's abuse of this freedom (*BLW* 46–47). He notes that Adam could choose to remain in God's will or abandon it (*BLW* 133). He approvingly cites Augustine to say that Adam had the grace of free will to choose the good, and that the freedom that existed before it was lost by the fall included the possibility of choosing the good or the evil (*BLW* 177–78). These observations certainly affirm the power of contrary choice before the fall. It appears that Calvin would agree with me about the implications of Genesis 2:16–17.

Although the passage, as I have acknowledged, does not prove freedom *after* the fall, it does show that freedom was part of the constitution of humanity made in the image of God. And I must raise this question: if the dialogue between God and unfallen Adam was appropriate for freedom of choice, then should we not consider similar exchanges made subsequently, with similar instructions and options presented, as indicating the same thing? At the least, we ought to examine carefully the subsequent situations that the Bible puts before us, situations where human choice is assumed or stated.

The Objectors' Treatment of Such Passages

Before I survey some typical passages of Scripture that support the human capacity of free will, I choose first to deal with the way Luther, Calvin, and Edwards answer such claims as I am about to make. As a class, these passages indicate that choices for or against God are set before human beings with the implications that either choice is open to them. To one after another of these Luther and Calvin, especially (Edwards's approach is different), respond in a fairly consistent and similar way. By discussing these together now, I will be able to avoid some needless repetition when treating specific passages.

Many of the passages set forth God's *commands* to humankind, which we may also refer to as God's *law*. People who uphold free will often argue that the giving of a command implies the ability to obey it, and so freedom of choice. (I would agree only that there is some validity to this, but it is an argument that must be used carefully if at all.) Luther and Calvin respond to such arguments, generally, with three closely related observations: (1) that the purpose of God's law is to reveal sin rather than to provide for its cure; (2) that the law of God serves to reveal our duty and not our ability; and (3) that God's law convinces us of our inability to live in subjection to God.

Thus, when confronted with Deuteronomy 30, for example, Luther cites Romans 3:20: "By the law is knowledge of sin." Then he observes that, according to Paul, the law does nothing but "make sin known"; such passages show our duty, not our ability, and are given to make us know our inability, but they "do not prove the power of 'free-will'" (*BW* 158, 165).

An aside here seems appropriate and has some bearing on this discussion. Luther is famous for sharply distinguishing, throughout Scripture, between law and gospel (or grace). At the risk of some oversimplification, I observe that for him all commands are *law* and all promises are *grace*. Consequently, he rebukes Erasmus for not distinguishing the two. Erasmus had cited a group of passages that urge people to *turn* to God, including Zechariah 1:3; Jeremiah 15:19; and Ezekiel 18:23. He had also cited Isaiah 1:19, "If you are willing and obedient, you shall eat the good of the land." Luther calls Isaiah 1:19 *law* and the others *gospel*, "by which the afflicted and broken-hearted are summoned to consolation by the word that offers grace" (*BW*

163). He characterizes Ezekiel 18:23 as the gospel, "the sweetest consolation to miserable sinners," indicating that more than half the Bible consists in "mere promises of grace, by which mercy, life, peace and salvation are offered by God to men" (*BW* 167). For Luther, the Lord's statement "I desire not the death of a sinner" "is concerned only to proclaim and offer to the world the mercy of God"; those who receive it are "those in whom the law has already completed its fork, that is, given knowledge of sin" (*BW* 169).

Interestingly, Luther goes on to say that "turn," in Scripture, is used in two ways: (1) in a legal sense, where it requires "a change in the whole life" (as in Jeremiah 25:5; 35:15; 4:1) and includes all the commandments; and (2) in an evangelical sense, where "it is an utterance of divine consolation and promise, by which nothing is required of us, but the grace of God is offered to us," as in Psalms 14:7; 126:1 (*BW* 165–66). Perhaps Luther, then, would regard *some* of the passages I will offer as gospel instead of law, but it is not clear what criteria he would use to determine which is which.

Calvin offers no such distinctions, but he is consistently clear in his view of passages that appear to present humankind with a choice between obedience and disobedience. Citing Romans 3:20, he observes that God's law does "nothing except for making . . . sin plain." He adds that Romans 5:20, which says that the law entered to make sin abound, "would not be true if any power to obey existed in man" (*BLW* 166). Subsequently, he cites Romans 7:9 to say that the result of the law is "to kill"; he insists that he does not allow anyone "to deduce from commandments the extent or nature of human ability to obey" (*BLW* 206).

Calvin does make a connection between law and grace. He mentions that in his *Institutes* he had said that the law shows our duty, "so that one should ask the Lord urgently for the power to obey" (*BLW* 167) and "rest on God's strength, not his own" (*BLW* 208). Thus he sees Deuteronomy 30:11–14, in the light of Romans 10:5–9, as illuminating "a pathway to the gospel" that therefore "has the function of leading people to Christ" (*BLW* 169).

A brief critique of Luther and Calvin in this matter will serve to help the reader understand my usage of the passages to follow in this chapter. I am convinced that their response to these passages is inadequate as a result of drawing too-fine definitions of the things God says to human beings. Certainly, when God "lays down the law," so to speak, that alone does not prove that fallen humans have the ability to obey without a work of God's grace within them. Yes, by the law is the knowledge of sin (Romans 3:20), but that is not to say that this is the whole or *only* divinely intended function of the law. Galatians 3:24 speaks of yet another function. Both Luther and Calvin acknowledge that the law works in some people a sense of need for God's help. Furthermore, the law provides a revelation of the character of God and his ideal design for human behavior.

I have no desire here to pursue the manifold functions of the law of God, but I do mean to say that God's expression of his will by which people are to live is not of such a nature that one can pick out this verse and that verse and categorize it as *law*, and then dispose of it handily because it is there for the specific purpose of showing the hearers their sinfulness and inability to live up to it. I would submit that any objective reading of the passages I am about to treat below must at least consider the likely possibility that the Lord was dealing with the people about things they could reasonably be expected to do, *in at least some conceivable way*—a qualification that requires careful attention. The passages make best sense when read in that light. If someone should answer that this would require sinless perfection of humans, I would respond with a simple denial and a question: where in the Bible are God's blessings withheld from all but those who are sinless?

To be more specific about this, I would suggest that the passages I will discuss in the rest of this chapter should be regarded neither as *law* alone nor (to use Luther's distinction) as *promise/gospel/grace* alone, but as *gracious invitations* that incorporate both law and gospel. In the entire biblical story, God repeatedly invites human beings to be in fellowship with him and experience his blessings. He does that without expecting perfection. But he does expect repentance and commitment. And in his invitations he offers that possibility.

Is it possible for fallen human beings to repent of sin and commit to God? No. Not as they are, left to themselves. But the Word of God, spoken to human beings by the living Spirit of God, does not leave them to themselves. Yes, fallen persons are depraved and dead, blind and bound by sin, but the quickening, enlightening Word of grace both invites them and enables them to respond without necessitating a yes or a no, but making either response the possible choice of the sinner.

I will not expand on this now but refer the reader to chapter 8, which deals with free will, depravity, and grace. In my comments on the passages to follow, however, the reader will recognize that when I speak of the "winds of grace" blowing, this enabling, gracious invitation of God is what I am referring to.

Old Testament Passages

God and Cain

After the fall, after universal and disabling depravity, God spoke to Cain in Genesis 4:6–7, when Cain apparently brought less than the best he had as a gift in worship of God and God rejected his gift:

> So the Lord said to Cain, Why are you angry? And why has your countenance fallen? If you do well, will you not be accepted? And if you do not do well, sin lies at the door.

The natural way to read this is that God gave Cain two alternatives and the freedom to choose between them. To be sure, our freedom lies only within the boundaries God sets; it is God who gives and defines freedom.

The objection to this is that Cain was depraved—spiritually dead and deaf and blind and bound—and could not respond to God's offer to choose submission to him. I say that when God said "If you do well," his words, given life and power by the Spirit, enabled Cain to respond positively in spite of his depravity, and that the biblical account makes the best sense in this light.

The sweet winds of grace were blowing then, and God was offering Cain the way to forgiveness and life: to submit to God or reject him. Tragically, he expressed his choice in spilling the blood of his innocent brother, whose offering God had accepted.

Freedom is a fierce thing!

Leviticus 26 and Obedience versus Disobedience in Israel

There are many *ifs* in the Bible, and they often set alternatives before us. These alternatives are the way freedom of choice is expressed. When we get to Leviticus 26, the alternatives are summed up clearly. The first is in verses 3–13:

> If you walk in My statutes, and keep My commandments, and perform them . . . I will walk among you and be your God, and you shall be My people.

In verses 14–39 the other alternative appears:

> But if you do not obey Me, and do not observe all these commandments, and if you despise My statutes, or if your soul abhors My

judgments, so that you do not perform all my commandments, but break My covenant.

If they choose that alternative, the Lord will set his face against them (verse 12), and walk contrary to them (verse 24), bring the land into desolation (verse 32), and scatter them among the heathen (verse 33).

Must we take this passage to mean something other than what it says? Should we ignore its obvious implications? Did God mean for his hearers to see, when he offered this, that there was no way they could do what he asked, and so the two alternatives were not both open to them in any way at all? Should they have responded—as some dispensationalists have suggested the Israelites should have responded at Sinai when given the Mosaic covenant—by throwing up their hands and saying, "We cannot do this. Give us something different"?

The passage does not lend itself to a neat distinction between law and gospel. There are commands referred to, for sure. But there are promises, too. Two ways of life were being set before Israel, with the clear implication that they must choose between them and that the promised blessings would be theirs if they chose the path of obedience.

Who will read such a passage—and the Bible has many like it—and say that it does not clearly speak to the possibility of choice? The obvious purpose of the passage was to put the responsibility on Israel to choose between the alternatives God set before them, to bless them if they chose to obey and to curse them if they chose the way of disobedience. If we do not learn this from the whole example of Israel in the wilderness and in Canaan, what do we learn? Paul says that all this was written for our instruction (1 Corinthians 10:11).

Does the inability of depraved humanity mean that God was speaking tongue-in-cheek, intending not to urge them to walk in his ways but to convince them that they could not do so? Before drawing this conclusion, listen again to the first alternative: "If you will walk in my ways then I will walk among you and be your God and you will be my people." I suggest that this covenant language represented a real offer, and that once again the sweet winds of grace were blowing. God's word to Israel was more than a powerless command to do what they could not do; instead, it was a gracious invitation. He was offering grace, and setting the right way before them, so that they could see it in spite of their blindness, thus enabling the response God desired.

Moses's Parting Words to Israel in Deuteronomy

While there is no need to multiply passages relating to God's dealings with Israel, what Moses said to the children of Israel as he prepared to part from them is especially important and revealing. Consider Deuteronomy 11:26–28:

> Behold, I set before you today a blessing and a curse: the blessing, if you obey the commandments of the Lord your God, which I command you today; and the curse, if you do not obey the commandments of the Lord your God, but turn aside from the way which I command you today, to go after other gods, which you have not known.

Moses takes this up again in Deuteronomy 30:11–20, his final warning.

> For this commandment which I command you today, it is not too mysterious for you, nor is it far off. . . . The word is very near you, in your mouth and in your heart, that you may do it. See, I have set before you today life and good, death and evil, in that I command you today to love the Lord your God, to walk in his ways, and to keep his commandments; . . . and the Lord your God will bless you. . . . But if your heart turns away so that you do not hear, and are drawn away, and worship other gods, and serve them, I announce to you today that you shall surely perish. . . . I call heaven and earth as witnesses today against you, that I have set before you life and death, blessing and cursing; therefore choose life, that both you and your descendants may live.

The words and their implications seem clear enough. Moses speaks for God and says, "I offer you a choice. You can be blessed or cursed. Choose to obey God and you choose the blessing. Choose to turn away from His ways and you choose the curse." That is freedom of choice, and it speaks as clearly as if the written word had said directly that fallen humanity has freedom of will. If those Moses addressed did not have the power to choose between those alternatives, his words seem to be cruel mockery. Can we really think God would tantalize them with a choice they could not make? That his command was nothing more than a reminder of what they ought but could not do?

No. In fact, Moses said the command was *not* hidden from them; it was *not* out of their reach. When God gave them the first alternative—to love him and walk in his ways—he was not dangling blessing and good and life before them to remind them how far they were from it. Instead, in his words, given life by the Spirit of God, the sweet winds of grace were blowing again, and he was not just offering them blessing but inviting and enabling them to choose.

I am not negating depravity or the inability of people to choose for God if left to themselves. But the Word of God, conveyed to the heart by the Spirit of God, does not leave people to themselves. Words like these which Moses spoke to Israel are instruments of grace. It was law, but it was not *mere* law. It was gospel, but it was not *mere* gospel. It was an invitation to grace conveyed in grace, and it did not leave the hearers unable to respond.

By the way, the Hebrew verb for *choose* occurs far more often in Deuteronomy than in any other book in the Old Testament—thirty-one times in all. The interesting thing is that in thirty of those thirty-one times it refers to *God's* choices. Over and over we read the words "the Lord your God shall choose." Does God have free will? Certainly so. Is it any surprise, then, that his image-bearer also has free will?

This challenge of Moses went a step farther. In verse 29 he said that when the Israelites would later come into possession of the land under Joshua's leadership, they should put the blessing he pronounced on Mt. Gerizim and the curse he pronounced on Mt. Ebal. In Deuteronomy 27 he gave instructions about this. So we read in Joshua 8 that this is exactly what happened. They parked the ark of the covenant in the valley floor between the two mountains, and half the Israelites stood on one side of the ark at the foot of Mt. Gerizim while half of them stood on the other side at the foot of Mt. Ebal. And then Joshua read the law of God and the blessings God had pronounced on those who obey, and the people on Mt. Gerizim said amen. And then he read all the curses God had pronounced on disobedience, and the people on Mt. Ebal said amen.

Here were the two alternatives, and here was their choice. If they could not do that at all, what point did the drama have? Was it a macabre play, after all, on the surface offering life but with a hidden meaning to say that they were dead people without hope? Such a twisted reading goes exactly counter to the obvious reading.

In fact, Israel *could* do what God was asking, if the situation is understood rightly and in accord with an understanding of how God works. The gracious Word of God, wafted along by the Spirit of God, gave them understanding of the choice, gave them to see that they should and could choose God's way. God Almighty was speaking to offer himself to fallen humankind, inviting them to fellowship with him. And by that Spirit-breathed offer he was enabling them to accept or reject him. And some of them did the one and some did the other.

We must take this passage yet one step further. In Romans 10:6–8 Paul cites from these words of Moses (Deuteronomy 30:12–14) and applies them to New Testament salvation by faith. He says that the "word" Moses gave (in verse 14) is, in fact, the "word of faith which we preach"; in other words, the gospel. He applies the passage directly to "the righteousness of faith," so much so that it is this righteousness that is "speaking" in Deuteronomy. Indeed, he stresses the purpose of Moses' words to show that this righteousness is *not* somewhere out of reach or difficult to attain, but is as near as one's mouth and heart—a mouth capable of confession and a heart capable of faith.

The commentary of C. F. Keil on this passage in Deuteronomy observes,

> However near the law had thus been brought to man, sin had so estranged the human heart from the word of God, that doing and keeping the law had become . . . impossible; so that the declaration, "the word is in thy heart," only attains its full realization through the preaching of the gospel of the grace of God, and the righteousness that is by faith; and to this the Apostle Paul applies the passage in Rom. x. 25 sqq. [sic].[1]

The comment is judicious. But if human beings in the Old Testament could be saved, and if salvation was by faith then as now—both of which seem obvious—then Paul is right to indicate that the gospel was already wrapped up in Moses's words. To be sure, the specific form faith took in the Mosaic system was different from the form it takes now, but the principle or substance was the same. And Moses was preaching the gospel as well as the law, and the gracious word of invitation to fellowship with God, applied to hearts by the Spirit of God, made it possible for the hearers to respond in faith. Even then, the "word" was as near as their mouths and hearts, put there within the reach of faith by the Word of God and the Spirit of God. I would suggest that the winds of grace were blowing as surely as they are now when redemption is preached under the convicting work of the Spirit.

I have yet one more observation, of a more technical and grammatical nature, about these passages in Deuteronomy. There is a specific construction in the Hebrew original here, which I may summarize as the verb *nathan* (give, place) plus the preposition *l* (before) prefixed to a form of *panim* (face, person), translated "I have set before you," *followed by options*. It appears in 11:26; 30:1; and 30:15. That precise construction, with two options

---

1. Keil and Delitzsch, *Genesis to Judges* 6:32, 1107.

as objects of the verb, occurs only once more in the Old Testament: namely, in Jeremiah 21:8, "I set before you the way of life and the way of death." In this case, the options were to go out in submission to Nebuchadnezzar and live, or to remain in the city of Jerusalem, resisting, and die. I think it highly unlikely that any interpreter would suggest that Jeremiah's hearers could not make either of the choices. What seems likely is that the very construction was intended to suggest what we may call "live" options, when the persons so challenged were able to choose either. And it seems equally likely that this is the implication of the construction in Deuteronomy, when the persons so challenged were enabled to choose between life and death, blessing and cursing, which God set before them.

Joshua's Farewell Message

Moses's successor Joshua also delivered a farewell message to the children of Israel. Although it introduces nothing new to the discussion, it is pointed enough to bear at least a brief mention, as recorded in Joshua 24:14–15:

> Now therefore, fear the Lord, serve him in sincerity and in truth, and put away the gods which your fathers served on the other side of the River and in Egypt. Serve the Lord! And if it seems evil to you to serve the Lord, choose for yourselves this day whom you will serve, whether the gods which your fathers served that were on the other side of the River, or the gods of the Amorites, in whose land you dwell. But as for me and my house, we will serve the Lord.

It is difficult to see how free will could be any more plainly exposed, at least if one assumes that the enabling grace of God was at work. Joshua spoke for God and challenged the people to choose. And in Joshua's words of invitation and in his own stated example, the sweet winds of grace were blowing to enable the people to choose.

"Choose ye," said Joshua.

"We have chosen," they said.

I repeat, lest it be forgotten, that I am not denying their depravity, or their spiritual deadness or inability. I am saying that just as Jesus and Peter and Paul said to impotent men, "Stand up and walk," and the gracious, inviting word of command enabled them to do so, so Joshua's challenge to the people was the kind that enabled them to make the choice.

New Testament Passages

The New Testament reads the same as the Old. Here are just a few examples.

Jesus' Call to His First Disciples

Consider the call of the first disciples in Matthew 4. Jesus was walking by the Sea of Galilee and observed Peter and Andrew as they were fishing. "Come, follow me, and I will teach you to fish for men," he said. And his word itself, heard as the gracious invitation it was by the breath of the Spirit on their hearts, enabled them to choose between the family fishing business and being disciples of Jesus. By grace God enabled them to choose, yet it was their choice, after all. Later, Peter would say, "*We* have left all and followed you."

A General Invitation

Indeed, the New Testament sets before us the same kind of *ifs*, the same kind of alternatives that we find in the Old Testament. Hear Jesus himself saying in Matthew 10:32–33,

> *Whoever confesses Me before men, him I will also confess before My Father who is in heaven. But whoever denies Me before men, him I will also deny before My Father who is in heaven.*

This is, by the way, the choice of eternal life versus eternal death, and Jesus expressed it in the two alternatives.

To be sure, depraved, dead, deaf, disabled sinners cannot do this merely by their free will. But again, in the words of Jesus the sweet winds of grace are blowing, and he is offering himself to those who will receive him, and those who hear this generous invitation breathed to them by the Holy Spirit of God are thereby enabled to respond—or not.

The Rich Young Ruler

In some instances people who were given the opportunity chose *not* to follow Jesus. The account of the rich young ruler appears in Matthew 19:16–22 as well as in Mark 10:17–27 and Luke 18:18–27. "What shall I do to inherit eternal life?" he asked, and Jesus answered him directly. "Cut all the ties," he said, "renounce every other master, including especially the master Mammon that controls your life, and come be my disciple; follow me."

Every reader knows the outcome: he went away in sorrow. He chose his possessions over Jesus. "There you have it," someone says, "he was depraved and dead, unable to respond to Jesus' challenge." I think not. I do not think Jesus would have challenged him to do what he could not do just to show him that he could not. I do not think that the heart of Jesus would have reached out in love, as Mark tells us was happening here, if the young man was wholly consumed with unrelieved evil and hatred for God.

Instead, we should read the passage in its plainest sense. When Jesus called the young man to choose him instead of his riches, the sweet winds of grace were blowing. Just as Peter commanded the dead Dorcas to get up from her bier, and she could, so Jesus' words, breathed into the young man by the Spirit of God, made it possible for him to choose Jesus and life. Instead, he chose his money and eternal death. He really could have chosen the other way. I repeat: free will is a fierce and terrible thing.

Jesus' Lament over Jerusalem

I cite the sad words of Matthew 23:37, as Jesus approached Jerusalem for the last time:

> O Jerusalem, Jerusalem! . . . How often I wanted to gather your children together, as a hen gathers her chicks under her wings, but you were not willing!

"It was my will to draw you to myself," he said, "but your will was not to allow me." "Of course they *would* not," one says, "they *could* not!" I do not believe that is a realistic way to read the passage. I cannot believe Jesus would have expressed himself this way if that had been the case. No, the point is that Jesus had come to them as the very revelation of God in himself, and he had taught in their streets and in their synagogues and in the temple courts, sharing the truth of God. He had worked miracles before their eyes, feeding thousands from a few loaves and fish, restoring withered hands, raising some from death, curing incurable leprosy, giving sight and speech and hearing to the blind and dumb and deaf. Indeed, then, the sweet winds of grace had been blowing all about Jerusalem.

"But they were depraved and dead and deaf and disabled," one says. Yes, and left to themselves, they made the only choice they could: to turn deaf ears to the truth and blind eyes to the work of God in their midst. But they were not left to themselves. Jesus was there and his life-giving word was there and the breath of the Spirit of God was there. And every single inhabitant of Jerusalem *could* have listened and seen and understood and chosen to turn to God. Those powerful, gracious words and works made it possible. And some of them did, and some of them did not. And there was their free will.

Conclusion

These examples could be multiplied at length; there is not space to expound the whole Bible here. See, the Bible does not spend its time saying that God created humankind with freedom of will or defining what free will is. What the Bible does, from one cover to the other, is to give us one example after another of free will in practice. Free will is on nearly every page. The whole drama is about God and humanity and freedom of will.

Why else would Jesus warn that you cannot serve two masters (Matthew 6:24)? One must choose one or the other.

Why else would Jesus speak woe to the cities of Chorazin and Bethsaida, saying that if the mighty works he did in those two cities had been done in Tyre and Sidon they would have repented long ago (Mark 11:20)?

Why else did he warn his seventy disciples that, as they went about preaching, some people would receive them and other people would not receive them, and in the latter case they should shake the dust from their feet and move on (Luke 10:8)?

Why else did John say that Jesus came to his own and his own rejected him, but those who received him in faith he made sons of God (John 1:12)?

What other than freedom of will could Jesus be talking about when he said to some of his hearers, "You are not willing to come to Me that you may have life" (John 5:40)? This is not a prediction or a mere statement of fact; it is a strong rebuke, implying a wrong choice made when they did not have to do so.

What other than free choice was happening on the hill Calvary when one thief repented and made Paradise his destiny while the other persisted in mockery of the man dying to make grace available to them both (Luke 13:39)?

What other than free will was happening in the synagogue at Antioch in Pisidia when Paul had preached the gospel and some responded in faith but others responded in contradiction and blasphemy, and Paul said, "It was necessary that the word of God should be spoken to you first; but since you reject it and judge yourselves unworthy of everlasting life, behold we turn to the Gentiles" (Acts 13:46)?

What else but free will was involved when Paul, preaching at a pagan temple in Athens, said that God commands all persons everywhere to repent (Acts 17:30)? All people? Everywhere? Then apparently Jesus provided for them all and all of them, when they hear the gracious gospel invitation under the gracious persuasion of God's Spirit, can obey.

What else but free will is involved when Luke, at the end of Acts, reports that, in response to Paul's proclamation in Rome, "Some believed the things which were spoken, and some believed not" (Acts 28:24)?

And what else but free will is involved in all those *whoever* passages?

- "For God so loved the world that he gave his only begotten Son, that *whoever* believes in him should not perish but have everlasting life." (John 3:16)

- "*Whoever* drinks of the water that I shall give him will never thirst. But the water that I shall give him will become in him a fountain of water springing up into everlasting life." (John 4:14)

- "*Whoever* calls on the name of the Lord shall be saved." (Acts 2:21)

- And almost the last words of the Bible: "*Whoever* desires, let him take the water of life freely." (Revelation 22:17)

This sounds to me like open salvation, not closed salvation. And open salvation means freedom of choice. Only do not forget that the winds of grace blow in every one of these sweet invitations, and by that grace every dead, depraved, deaf, and disabled sinner who hears the gracious invitation and is breathed on by the Spirit and sees the light of the gospel is made able to exercise the latent power of free will—and so to believe and be saved or to reject and be damned forever. Yes, free will is a fierce freedom, indeed.

Much, much more could be added, as anyone who knows the Scriptures realizes. But this is a large enough sample to make the biblical picture clear. From Genesis to Revelation, the story is about God and humanity and how they relate. About how God created human beings and gave them the choice between life and death, and how they chose death for the whole human race. About how the God whose nature is not just holiness but also redemptive love continued to deal in grace with humankind and provide salvation for them all, by his gracious and Spirit-empowered invitation making it possible for dead persons, though deaf and blind, to hear and see and understand and so to believe or disbelieve.

Part Two

The Case against Free Will

4

Martin Luther against Free Will

MARTIN LUTHER (1483–1546), A German monk, ignited the Protestant
Reformation—although that was not his immediate intention—in October
1517 when he published his Ninety-Five Theses to protest abuses in the
Roman Church's sale of indulgences. At the time, having completed his
doctorate in theology at the University of Wittenberg in 1512, he was a
professor there, teaching biblical interpretation and doctrine.

Luther's studies, as well as his reading of Augustine, had brought him
to the doctrine of justification by faith alone, which would thereafter be
at the heart of his theology and of his conflict with the Roman Church.
Gradually, his differences with the church grew to include challenges to the
infallibility of the pope and church councils, to the church's sacramental
system, to the doctrine of transubstantiation, and to the sacrificial Mass.
Even so, he continued to press for reforms within the church rather than for
the founding of a separate church.

At the end of 1520, however, Luther was condemned by the Roman
hierarchy and excommunicated by the pope. At the famous Diet (a formal
assembly) in Worms, Germany, in 1521, he refused to recant. The emperor
banned him and directed that all his writings be burned. He spent most of
the rest of his life in Wittenberg, writing, teaching, and assisting with the
reforms that were taking place. He died in 1546.[1]

Luther's volume against freedom of the will was written in direct response to a book published in 1524 entitled *Diatribe on Free Will*. It was
written by Desiderius Erasmus, an older contemporary of Luther. Erasmus had at first encouraged Luther but subsequently broke with him and

---

1. For a brief and helpful article about Luther, see Heinze, "Luther, Martin."

remained loyal to the Roman Catholic establishment. He was a classical scholar, called a "Christian humanist" by many. Like Luther, he thought some church reforms were needed, but he believed the best way to do that was by "the application of humanistic scholarship to Christian tradition."[2] Among many other things, he is noted for his publication of the first Greek New Testament, which was the basis for what became known as the "Received Text" (*Textus Receptus*). His work in support of free will probably represented his final break with Luther.

Luther's answer appeared in print in 1525, entitled *De Servo Arbitrio* (*On the Bondage of the Will*). In my treatment of Luther, then, I will be interacting specifically with the English translation of this famous publication (cited in the text as *BW*).

Luther versus Erasmus: An Overview

Erasmus was defending what he understood to be the established view of the Roman Catholic Church in favor of the freedom of the will. That put him at odds with Luther, whose volume is divided into eight parts, including the introduction and conclusion. I do not propose to provide a detailed account of the exchange between the two men, but for the reader's sake I offer a summary of each of the eight parts. In doing so I accept Luther's representations of Erasmus's views at face value, since—even if he were not entirely accurate in these—it makes no difference in my own interaction with Luther. I am certainly not taking Erasmus's side in the debate.

Part I (*BW* 62–65): Introduction. This includes no joining of the issues.

Part II (*BW* 66–108): Review of Erasmus' Preface. Erasmus had begun with some preliminary observations: (1) He found dogmatic assertions to be distasteful and included a definition of free will among those, a stance that Luther disdained, insisting that one must know what the so-called free will is capable of. (2) He had thought some Scripture passages obscure, while Luther insisted on the perspicuity of Scripture. (3) He had said it is vain to argue about God's foreknowledge and how contingency and necessity are related. Luther maintained that any treatment of free will must include discussion of these matters. (4) He had said that some matters, being paradoxes, ought not be publicly discussed lest the result be destructive to the church, and Luther rebuked him for this, insisting that difficult truths serve to humble people and that items of faith are by nature hidden and

---

2. Clouse, "Erasmus, Desiderius," 361.

paradoxical. (5) He had discounted the idea that everything we do is by necessity rather than by free will. Luther responded that apart from salvation people do evil by nature and necessarily, and that not we but God alone works salvation in us. (6) He had said that the power of human will is small and ineffective without grace, which Luther insisted was equivalent to saying that the will is not free.

Part III (BW 109–36): Review of Erasmus' Introduction. Erasmus's main points were these: (1) The church fathers disagreed with Luther, who replied that this is not entirely true and does not really matter. (2) It is hard to believe that God has allowed the church, in its insistence on free will, to be wrong for so long if Luther were right. Luther responded that the visible church is not the true church, which is hidden from humanity's view and does not err. (3) Some Scripture passages are ambiguous and unclear, but Luther affirmed that only the Scriptures can stand as a basis for judgment, and they are clear to those who are spiritually minded. He noted that the blindness of humanity does not disprove this clarity.

Part IV (BW 137–89): Review of Erasmus' Arguments for Free Will. (1) Erasmus had defined free will to mean that a person has power to apply himself to or to turn from things that lead on to salvation. Luther countered that Erasmus had credited the will with too much, that spiritual things cannot even be discerned by natural human beings (1 Corinthians 2:9), much less can they turn toward God. He continued to criticize Erasmus for failing to indicate *what* a person can do by free will. (2) Erasmus had acknowledged that humanity cannot do good apart from the help of grace. Luther observed that this in effect contradicted Erasmus's definition just given and insisted that human beings can will nothing good until God is in them. (3) Erasmus had cited God's commandments and humanity's obligations to God as evidence of human ability. Luther replied that commandments only show human beings their impotence, and obligations do not indicate ability to meet them. (4) Erasmus had cited passages like Deuteronomy 30:19 that challenge people to choose between good and evil as proving their ability. Luther cited Romans 3:20, "By the law is the knowledge of sin." He also chided Erasmus for having professed to believe in a will that needs grace when in fact his insistence on humanity's ability would prove that grace was not needed. And he observed that Erasmus had not distinguished between law and grace. (5) Erasmus had objected that God could not deplore the death of those whose death he had willed. Luther responded by distinguishing between God's revealed will and his secret, inscrutable will: we cannot know the reasons God has not revealed something and must not attempt to pry into them. (6) Erasmus had set forth that people's good and bad works cannot be by necessity, else there would be no grounds for punishment and reward. Luther responded that New Testament commands to godliness are for those who are already justified, and that reward is based on God's promise, not merit. (7) Erasmus had protested that our works are not ours if they are of necessity. Luther answered that necessity does not destroy moral responsibility. He also said, again, that Erasmus was proving more than he claimed and so showing human ability without grace rather than as enabled by grace.

Part V (BW 190–238): Review of Erasmus' Treatment of Texts that Deny Free Will (I). Luther showed that Erasmus avoided various passages of Scripture (1) by finding unwarranted figures of speech in them; (2) by merely affirming what he thought they mean without giving evidence; (3) by distorting how God does such things as working evil in or hardening persons—as in the case of Pharaoh's heart; (4) by avoiding the logic that if God foreknows the future acts of people those acts are done "of necessity" and foreknowledge cannot be falsified by human decisions—as in the case of Judas's betrayal, where Erasmus (to Luther's mind) confused necessity and compulsion; (5) by pretending that passages like Malachi 1:2–3, as treated in Romans 9:11–13, deal with matters of standing and privilege rather than salvation; and (6) by attributing something other than the obvious meaning to passages dealing with the potter and the clay, as in Romans 9:20ff. Again, Luther chided Erasmus for having claimed, earlier, to believe that human will requires the assistance of grace, when his arguments would sustain the power of the will without the need for grace.

Part VI (BW 239–72): Review of Erasmus' Treatment of Texts that Deny Free Will (II). Luther argued against the way Erasmus had dealt with important passages that expose humanity's bondage to sin, including Genesis 6:3; 8:21; and 6:5; Isaiah 40:1–2, 6–7; Jeremiah 10:23; Proverbs 16:1; 21:1; and John 15:5. Luther argued, from the last of these, that people are enslaved by Satan and yet under the general, providential control of God, as in John 3:27, so that God alone moves all things by his omnipotence and yet humanity cooperates or is made to act by God.

Part VII (BW 273–318): The Bible Doctrine of the Bondage of the Will. Luther undertook to show from various passages—especially in Romans and John—that the Bible teaches human inability to will for God apart from the gracious work of God within: Romans 1:18ff; 3:9ff, 19ff; 3:21–26; 4:2–3; 8:5; 9:30–31; 10:20; John 1:5, 10–13; 3:1ff; 3:18, 36, 27, 31;

6:44; 8:23; 14:6 and others. He concluded the book with his own summary of his main arguments, which I will use below to describe his primary reasons for rejecting free will.

Part VIII (*BW* 319–20): Conclusion. Luther prayed that God would enlighten Erasmus.

Understanding Luther

The Concept of Free Will That Luther Was Resisting

In order to understand any person's argument, one must know what the person is arguing *against*, and this is true in the matter of Luther's resistance to the concept of human freedom of choice. He was, after all, arguing against Erasmus in particular, and his discussion has many references to Erasmus's position on the subject, including direct citations. Whether he understood or represented Erasmus correctly is beside the point, although I have no reason to question that. What matters is that Luther was arguing against the view he attributed to Erasmus.

It is difficult to pin down exactly, from Luther's volume, what Erasmus believed about human ability. His statements appear to suggest two contradictory things. On the one hand, he certainly said that the will is not capable of doing good except with the assistance of grace. He distinguished three views involving the will: (1) those who deny that human beings can will good without special grace; (2) those who say humanity is "free" only to sin; and (3) those who say that free will is meaningless and God works both good and evil in people. Erasmus insisted that the first was his view (*BW* 144–45). He acknowledged that free will is "wholly ineffective apart from the grace of God" (*BW* 104).

At the same time, Erasmus attributed to free will some power, even if "small" (*BW* 104). He insisted that it has power enough to enable a person to "apply himself" either to turn toward or away from the "things that lead to eternal salvation" (*BW* 137). Indeed, using Ecclesiasticus 15:14–17, Erasmus said that God places before human beings a choice between life and death and gives them whichever pleases them (*BW*143). He compared a ship and helmsman, saying that "God preserves the ship, but the sailor steers it to harbor" (*BW* 267). He said that Genesis 4:7 shows that humans can overcome the motions of the mind toward evil and so do not sin of necessity (*BW* 156–57).

Luther's response to all this reveals what he was really opposing: namely, the notion that human beings have within themselves, apart from the gracious work of God in them, the power to apply themselves to good or to turn away from evil. He constantly chided Erasmus for claiming to believe that the will is not capable of good apart from grace, saying that Erasmus's insistence that the will has some power to turn toward God or away from sin really amounts to saying that humanity can act for good apart from grace. He also constantly interpreted Erasmus to mean that the will can act in this way "of itself," that it "moves itself by its own power" in the right direction (*BW* 140–42). For example, the way Erasmus used 2 Timothy 2:21, "If a man purge himself from these," convinced Luther that Erasmus saw in this a power that was effective without grace (*BW* 235).

Consequently, Luther's own definition of free will as his opponents saw it reveals what he was inveighing against. Commenting on John 3:18, for example, Luther—personifying free will—observed that if free will is one of those who believe then grace is not needed, "for of itself it believes on Christ" (*BW* 308). He warned that people think free will "means a power of freely turning in any direction, yielding to none and subject to none" (*BW* 105). He chided Erasmus for imagining that human will is "something placed in an intermediate position of 'freedom' and left to itself," so that it can make efforts "in either direction" (*BW* 262).

Ultimately, Luther was making war against the Roman Catholic conception of free will and human ability. He revealed this clearly when he said that "the protectors of 'free-will' deny Christ. . . . they have made Christ to be . . . a dreadful Judge, whom they strive to placate . . . by devising many works . . . by which they aim to appease Christ. . . . They do not believe that He intercedes before God and obtains grace for them by His blood" (*BW* 305).

Luther's Concept of the Human Will

Early in his resistance to Erasmus, Luther revealed what he took to be the issues involved in the discussion of free will: namely, (1) whether God "foreknows anything contingently"; (2) whether our wills are "active" or "merely passive" in the things of grace, that is, things "relating to eternal salvation"; and (3) whether our doing of good and evil, which are of necessity, are not rather "wrought in us" (*BW* 74). While he did not answer the questions here, the implications are clear enough: it is more correct to speak of what God does in us than of what we do.

Luther did go on to say that we cannot answer such questions without determining whether God "foreknows of necessity" (*BW* 79), thus signaling his answer. Nor does he leave it merely to be signaled, but proceeds almost immediately to add that Christians must understand that God "foresees, purposes, and does all things according to His own immutable, eternal and infallible will." This truth he calls a "bombshell" that "utterly shatters" free will (*BW* 80).

Unlike Calvin (as the next chapter will show), Luther did not take pains to distinguish humanity before and after the fall in this matter. He seemed content to speak of human beings in general, although one may assume he meant fallen human beings. Even so, he regarded the example of Adam as showing us what alone the will is capable of when left to itself (*BW* 156).

When Erasmus had objected to some of Augustine's views on the grounds that such views would mean that no wicked person would amend his ways, Luther responded that no person *could* ever amend his ways (*BW* 99). Indeed, all expressions of the law of God in Scripture were given for the purpose of showing us our inability to obey (*BW* 165, 288). Even so, he did not seem to be concerned to say this just because fallen humanity is depraved; instead, he was more concerned to establish the necessity of God's foreknowledge and predestination. The wicked person cannot will the good for the same reason that the regenerate person cannot will evil. Because God has worked in the regenerate, they will what is good, and here also there is no freedom of the will to do otherwise, "as long as the Spirit and grace of God remain in a man" (*BW* 103). He concluded this discussion with the analogy of a horse between two riders. If God or Satan ride (and they fight to see who does), the horse rides in the way that the rider wills.

Luther was much more likely to speak of Satan's influence, rather than corruption of nature, as in control of a wicked person. He said that either God or Satan is in us and therein lies the source of the will to choose good or evil, respectively (*BW* 147). Subsequently, he rebuked Erasmus for not believing that God and Satan are the "drivers of an *enslaved* will," with "each waging relentless war against the other!" (*BW* 262). Without grace, then, the will is not free but is "the permanent prisoner and bondslave of evil," entirely incapable of turning toward God (*BW* 104).

Luther would accept "free will" only as the power "which makes human beings fit subject to be caught up by the Spirit and touched by God's grace." He called this a "fitness, or 'dispositional quality' and 'passive aptitude'" that is unique to human beings, but he proceeded immediately to affirm that free will can only truly be attributed to God since he alone does "whatever he wills in heaven and earth" (Psalm 135:6) (*BW* 105). He concluded this particular discussion by observing that human beings have free will in respect to what is "below" them (as in money and possessions) but not to what is "above" them (anything related to God or that bears on salvation or damnation).

Instead, said Luther, every person is "a captive, prisoner and bond-slave, either to the will of God, or to the will of Satan" (*BW* 105). Even the distinction between what is "below" and what is "above," however, does not really lead to free will. Luther acknowledges that the will is "free" in the realm of *nature*, to do things like eating and drinking and begetting, although it is not in the realm of *grace*. Still, in the realm of nature, a person remains under "the general omnipotence of God who effects, and moves, and impels all things in a necessary, infallible course" (*BW* 265).

For Luther, then, there was no tolerance for speaking of free will. If Erasmus were to speak of "free will," he must say what that will was capable of, and he had not done so in any way that satisfied Luther. Such a will would have to enable a person to apply himself to grace, or to merit the Spirit or pardon for sins (*BW* 113). Otherwise, there is no "free will" fit for discussion. After emphasizing that everything God foreknows—and he foreknows everything—takes place by necessity, Luther says plainly, "This means that 'free-will' does not exist" (*BW* 222). Erasmus had claimed to follow a "middle way" in which he affirmed both free will and the need for grace. Luther insisted that if grace is needed, the reason is that free will can do nothing. He required Erasmus either to agree with the Pelagians and attribute everything to free will, or to join him and "deny 'free-will' altogether and ascribe everything to God" (*BW* 270).

Luther's Reasons for Rejecting Free Will

Luther himself summarized his objections to the views of Erasmus near the conclusion of his book (*BW* 317). He gave five considerations, which I will summarize more succinctly as four main objections to the free will view of Erasmus. In the whole volume, there may be other considerations against free will, but these are Luther's major ones, without which any others would be ineffective. These will provide the reader with an understanding of the primary considerations that weighed against free will in the mind of Luther—and the first receives the greatest attention because it loomed largest in his thinking and characterizes the entire volume.

One: The foreknowledge and predestination of God. Luther firmly believed that God foreknows and foreordains everything that takes place. In that case, he cannot be wrong and no one is "free" to make him wrong in what he has foreknown or to overturn what he has willed to occur. Consequently, "there can be no 'free-will'" (*BW* 317). He said that to attempt to establish both divine foreknowledge and human freedom would be to say that "contradictories do not clash" (*BW* 215).

This is straightforward enough, and it has a number of implications, two of them being especially important for understanding Luther. First, he equated foreknowledge and foreordination or predestination, a fairly common move among Reformed theologians. He insisted that what God is he is immutably, and this includes his knowledge, which is as immutable as his will, so that what he foreknows he wills and vice versa (*BW* 80).

Second, for Luther this meant, logically, that everything that transpires does so by *necessity*. Since God's will is eternal and changeless, nothing, regardless of how it appears to us, is done "mutably and contingently"; instead, everything takes place "necessarily and immutably in respect of God's will" (*BW* 80). Whatever is done must be done "where, when, how, as far as, and by whom" God foresees and wills (*BW* 81).

Luther used Judas for an example, saying that since God foreknew Judas's betrayal of Jesus, then he did so necessarily and could not have acted differently from what God had foreknown (*BW* 213). He called Erasmus and everybody to witness that if God cannot be mistaken in what he foreknows, then what he foreknows "must necessarily come to pass" (*BW* 213). Indeed, he anticipated that someone might cite human foreknowledge in objection, and so he made a clear distinction: if a person knows in advance that an eclipse will occur, and it does, it did not occur *because* it was foreknown by the person; instead, it was foreknown because it would occur. Not so with God (*BW* 213).

Furthermore, Luther linked with this logic the fact of God's *omnipotence*, which he defined as not merely God's ability to do things but "the active power by which He mightily works all in all" (*BW* 217). In other words, God's omnipotence means that he actively works all things immutably (*BW* 218). Consequently, once we admit the foreknowledge and omnipotence of God, we must admit that we act "under necessity" and not "by right of 'free-will'" (*BW* 218).

Luther did express some hesitations about the word *necessity*. At one point, he wished for a better word, and he proceeded to say that by it he did not mean *compulsion* (*BW* 81). He repeated this later and urged that the wicked person, left to himself, sins "spontaneously and voluntarily" even though of necessity (*BW* 102). He called this the "necessity of immutability," by which he apparently meant that facts cannot be changed. Erasmus had said, apparently, that "necessity has neither merit nor reward"; well, said Luther, if this meant the "necessity of compulsion," that is correct, but he was speaking about the "necessity of immutability," and so Erasmus was wrong (*BW* 181). In another place he used the words "necessity of force" and "necessity of infallibility" to make the same distinction, insisting that Judas sinned both willingly and necessarily and so his betrayal was "certainly and infallibly bound to take place" (*BW* 220).

At the same, time Luther made clear, repeatedly, that all events—good and evil—have been foreknown and foreordained by God, so that *necessity* really is necessity and a lesser word would not do as well. Obviously, he found no substitute for it. Indeed, he did not even entirely avoid the word *compulsion*; in his discussion of Romans 9:15–16, he observed that when God has willed our hardening we are "compelled to be hardened, willy-nilly!" (*BW* 215). He insisted that humans have the will God gave them and which God "makes to act by His own movement" (*BW* 258–59). Erasmus had interjected the idea of God's *permission* in such matters; Luther responded to say that whether one speaks of permission or not, people cannot avoid "the action of the omnipotent God by which all men's wills, good and bad, are moved to will and to act" (*BW* 259).

In summary, there are two closely related points here. One is that God's foreknowledge, *as knowledge*, cannot be overturned. That alone means that humanity is not free to act in any way different from what God has foreseen. The other is that God's foreknowledge exactly matches his predetermined will for the course of all things. This, too, means that humanity is not free to overturn the course of events God has foreordained.

Two: Human bondage either to Satan or to God. Luther tended to see human beings as existing in servitude, either to God or to Satan, mastered by one or the other of these two supernatural forces engaged in cosmic conflict. In one place he used the analogy of a horse caught between two riders, saying that if God or Satan ride—and they fight to see who does—then the horse rides the way the rider wills (*BW* 103). He delighted to insist that human beings are slaves in bondage either to God or to Satan (*BW* 105), that either God is in us to will only good or Satan is in us to will only evil (*BW* 147).

This means, then, that there is no free will for humankind: "You would not call a slave, who acts at the beck of his lord, *free*" (*BW* 137). To Erasmus's "middle way" Luther responded with pointed, rhetorical questions:

> Where then is our belief that Satan is the prince of this world, and reigns, as Christ and Paul tell us, in the wills and minds of men, who are his prisoners . . . ? Will this roaring lion, this restless, implacable enemy of the grace of God and the salvation of men, suffer man . . . to make endeavours towards good at any time, or . . . whereby he might escape Satan's tyranny? Will he not rather spur and urge man on to will and to do with all his power that which is contrary to grace? (*BW* 262)

It would appear, given the depth and breadth of Luther's claims, that his view that human beings are either under the rule of God or under the rule of Satan would apply to them in any condition, whether before or after the fall or before or after regeneration.

Three: Human bondage to sin (depravity). For Luther, even if Satan were not the slave master of sinful human beings, their own sinfulness holds them in bondage and negates the claims of free will. In a person who does not have the Spirit of God there is nothing "that can turn itself to good, but only to evil" (*BW* 317). Even if Satan did not have the human will in bondage, "sin itself, whose slave man is, would weigh it down enough to make it unable to will good" (*BW* 263).

Perhaps this did not play as large a part in Luther's volume as it did in Calvin's (see the next chapter), but the two Reformers were certainly in agreement that the corruption of fallen human nature negated any freedom humanity might have to turn to God. Luther interpreted Paul's description of all humankind as being "under sin" (Romans 3:9ff) to mean that the entire race are "slaves of sin" and thus left without any goodness (*BW* 278). He said that people act evilly because they cannot do otherwise and attributed this to a "corruption" of nature that "makes it impossible" for them to do otherwise (*BW* 205). He used Genesis 8:21 and 6:5 to argue that humanity is "wholly evil" (*BW* 243).

Four: The necessity of grace for overcoming evil. Luther strongly believed that any deliverance from sin that human beings experience must be solely the work of God's grace and grounded in the redemptive work of Jesus Christ alone. This meant, for him, that if the will is free to turn in that direction, then humanity must receive some of the credit. In making this point he used as a prime example (from Romans 9:30–31) the fact that the Jews "fell into unrighteousness" in spite of pursuing it "with all their powers," while the Gentiles, who pursued wickedness instead, received righteousness "by God's free gift" (*BW* 317).

Erasmus had professed to agree that humanity is not capable of good apart from grace. Luther, however, did not believe him, insisting that the abilities Erasmus thought people possess in themselves were such as did not require God's grace. Indeed, he said, in response to Erasmus, that if the will has no power apart from grace, then the will is therefore not free; take away grace and the will is capable only of evil (*BW* 104). For the will to be free, in other words, it must be able to turn itself toward God without his assistance.

Luther would agree to speak of the power of free will *only* if that meant being fit "to be caught up by the Spirit and touched by God's grace" (*BW* 105). But he saw grace as the very opposite of free will, saying that only those who speak "for grace against 'free-will'" should be the ones heeded as the true church (*BW* 123). Of himself and the other Reformers he said, "We shall do battle against 'free-will' for the grace of God" (*BW* 136). He chastised Erasmus for saying that "'free-will' can do nothing without grace" and yet in effect showing that "'free-will' can do all things without grace" (*BW* 160).

For Luther, God's grace must be the sole and effective cause of salvation. When God acts in grace to justify and deliver, the recipients of that grace "are made to act" by him, as indicated in Romans 8:14 (*BW* 267). He acknowledged that the works of human beings can be good if done "with the help of God's grace" but affirmed that to say this is to speak about the power of God's grace, not the power of free will, which can of itself do nothing (*BW* 269–70).

My purpose does not include critical interaction with Luther at this point. I will respond to his concerns in subsequent chapters, especially in the chapters on free will, foreknowledge, and necessity (7); on free will and the sovereignty and providence of God (9); and on free will, human depravity and the grace of God (8). Meanwhile, Luther was certainly right to resist the Roman view of free will defended by Erasmus. He was right to affirm the exhaustive foreknowledge and all-inclusive purpose of God; that fallen human beings are corrupt and unable of themselves to turn to God; and that salvation is the work of God and his grace, not in any sense something people achieve by their own efforts or deserving.

5

John Calvin against Free Will

JOHN CALVIN (1509–1564), BORN in France, is widely regarded as the leading systematic theologian of the Protestant Reformation. He was a second-generation Reformer, a lad of about eight years when Martin Luther in 1517 ignited the Reformation with his Ninety-Five Theses protesting abuses in the Roman church.

In 1536 Calvin issued the first edition of his *Institutes of the Christian Religion*, then a little volume of just six chapters. That work, his major contribution to Christian theology, would go through five editions, the last published in 1559 and having grown to seventy-nine chapters. The *Institutes*, originally written in Latin and translated into French by Calvin himself, were widely distributed throughout Europe at the time. No one would question their influence in reforming the theology of the Christian church. He wrote many other books, including commentaries on most of the Old Testament and all of the New Testament except Revelation. He spent the years of his preaching and writing ministry, from 1541 on, in Geneva, Switzerland, where he played a key role in bringing the Reformation to the church in that country.[1]

Like Luther, Calvin wrote his volume about free will in direct response to a specific book published in resistance to him and the other Reformers. The opposing author was Albert Pighius (c. 1490–1542), a Dutch Roman Catholic theologian, and his work, entitled *Ten Books on Human Free Choice and Divine Grace*, was published in 1542, reacting to the second edition (1539) of Calvin's *Institutes*. Of the ten "books" (or chapters), the first six were in answer to Calvin's chapter 2 and dealt with free will. The other four answered Calvin's chapter 8 and were on the subject of providence and predestination.

---

1. For a brief, helpful article on Calvin, see Reid, "Calvin, John."

In 1543, then, Calvin published his reply to Pighius, entitled *Defence of the Sound and Orthodox Doctrine of the Bondage and Liberation of Human Choice against the Misrepresentations of Albert Pighius of Kampen*. In this work Calvin dealt only with Pighius's first six chapters; he would later deal with the other four in a 1552 work entitled *Eternal Predestination of God*, at the same time responding to additional attacks by Jerome Bolsec.

In this chapter, and in this book, then, I am responding specifically to Calvin's reply to Pighius, published in English under the title *The Bondage and Liberation of the Will* (cited in the text as *BLW*).

Calvin versus Pighius: An Overview

My purpose does not include a detailed rehearsal or evaluation of the arguments between Calvin and Pighius. I have made careful summaries of every section in order to be sure that I understand Calvin's own views of free will and his reasons. Pighius was defending the doctrine of the Roman Catholic establishment and resisting the radical reforms that Luther and Calvin and others were instituting in the churches that were breaking away from Rome.

The discussion between Pighius and Calvin, in that mid-sixteenth century context, is not our discussion. I have no doubt that Pighius was wrong, in significant ways, in his conception of human ability. Calvin was right to accuse him of Pelagianism or (at best) semi-Pelagianism. In most of their exchanges, Calvin's logic and use of Scripture are superior to those of Pighius. Even so, for the reader's sake I will summarize the six main sections, assuming that Calvin's statements of Pighius's arguments are correct. (Even if they are not correct in some ways, my own interaction with Calvin will not be negatively affected by that.)

Book One (*BLW* 22–34). Pighius had said that the judgment of God is just *only* if we have free will and are able to obey or reject God's commandments. He criticized Luther (1) as having disregarded human reason in order to deny this; (2) as having said that freedom of choice, since the fall, is a name without substance and we are able only to sin; and (3) as having said that everything a person does is by necessity. He argued that if Luther were right, then (1) no one can prepare himself to receive God's grace; (2) human nature is corrupt and without value; (3) although we cannot keep the law God judges us for not doing so; (4) the "monstrous" doctrine of original sin would be right; and (5) even in their good works the righteous sin.

Calvin does not undertake to answer all these arguments at this point. He postpones, for example, the discussion of absolute necessity. He thinks Luther "exaggerated" in some ways (especially on the fifth point above), although with justification, and he defends Luther as "a distinguished apostle of Christ." He speaks especially to the fifth point, affirming that the natural powers of human beings by themselves cannot come to faith or obey God's law or attain true righteousness, and that whenever anyone hears the Word of God so as to obey it, God alone has performed this.

Book Two (*BLW* 35–86). Pighius had given seven arguments against the Reformers' doctrine that everything happens by necessity and is God's doing: (1) it removes all reason to attempt to do good; (2) it does away with justification for punishing crimes; (3) it cancels all reasons for political authority and instruction in doing good; (4) it denies religion and makes humans into brute beasts; (5) it makes God the author of all evil deeds; (6) it "damns the whole of nature," making humans entirely corrupt; and (7) it exposes God to ridicule. He had gone on to argue that none of the church fathers had understood Scripture in this way, citing a number of them as supporting free choice and insisting that it is right to cite tradition as well as Scripture since the Scriptures can easily be interpreted according to the interpreter's desires.

Calvin answers that while God in his sovereignty is in absolute control and everything happens by necessity, as he has ordained, yet human beings are liable for their sins because their corrupted nature—out of which all sins arise—is their own doing. Judging God to be the author of evil is a fleshly judgment about God's secret will. It is true that human nature is entirely corrupt, but this is a result of the fall and not of God's creative work in making humanity. As for the fathers, while a few of them might have supported human ability, most of them were ambiguous on the subject. Furthermore, Augustine was clearly on the side of the bondage of the fallen will, and for that matter the true source of authority is Scripture and not tradition.

Book Three (*BLW* 87–136). This section deals specifically with Augustine, whom Calvin had cited extensively in the *Institutes*. Pighius had resisted Calvin's claim that Augustine supported the Reformers' views. He accused Calvin of either quoting Augustine out of context or of misunderstanding him. He also proceeded to divide Augustine's writings into three main groups and to cite from each group in support of free will. He claimed that Augustine agreed with the rest of the fathers and tradition in this.

Calvin responds by showing that he had not quoted Augustine out of context or in misunderstanding, adding many more citations to prove his point. He accepts Pighius's three groups of Augustine's writings and proceeds to deal with each: (1) writings before the Pelagian controversy, (2) writings during that controversy, and (3) later writings. The first group were written against the Manichaean heresy, which attributed the evil in humanity to the creative work of God. Calvin shows that Augustine defended the freedom of the will *before the fall*, but agreed with the Reformers that fallen human nature is wholly corrupt. The second group were written against Pelagius and his followers, who asserted human ability to turn to God without grace. Indeed, Pighius had criticized Augustine, in these writings, for implying that necessity and freedom of choice can be in the same actions. Calvin asks "Why not?" and demonstrates that Augustine supported his view: namely, that God, by grace, moves the mind and will, as evil and corrupt as they are, to willing obedience. The third group were written later in Augustine's life. Calvin cites extensively to show that Augustine believed both that *we* will when we will what is good, and that God is the cause of this.[2]

Book Four (*BLW* 137–70). Pighius had set out to answer four "absurdities" he found in Calvin's *Institutes*, affirming his view: (1) that sin, to be sin, must be *voluntary*, and if it is *necessary*, it ceases to be sin; (2) that both virtues and vices derive from decisions freely made, else they could not be punished or rewarded; (3) that the fact that some fall away and some persevere shows the freedom to choose between good and evil; (4) that exhortations and warnings are in vain unless they can be heeded.

Calvin answers Pighius by making a number of points. (1) The necessity of sinning has resulted from the change of our nature that we brought on ourselves and is therefore blameworthy. (2) *Necessity* is not the same thing as *coercion*. (3) Even in doing good, we act while being acted on by God and so our wills are involved but only as changed by God. (4) On the basis of the free election of God, God both initiates the work and brings it to completion. (5) Exhortations and rebukes are spoken to those unable to obey but are also engraved in the hearts of those whom he regenerates.

Calvin also responds to Scriptures that Pighius had used against him, dividing them into three types. (1) Commandments, which Pighius said humans must be able to keep or else God is playing games with us. Calvin responds that the law serves to make our sins plain to us and cannot

---

2. See *BLW* 135–36 for Calvin's excellent summary of what Augustine taught that Calvin also held.

be obeyed from the heart unless God changes the heart. (2) Conditional promises, which Pighius said would have no purpose if we are unable to meet the conditions. Calvin observes that they show us our impotence and so prepare us to understand that God himself must gift us with meeting the conditions. (3) Statements that blame people for their failure to enjoy God's blessings, which Pighius says would be unfitting if those people were under a bondage to sin that they could not escape from. Calvin returns to the fact that human corruption is a result of human sin.

Book Five (*BLW* 171–201). Pighius had attacked the doctrine of the Reformers as (1) being in agreement with the Manichaeans that human nature is inherently evil and (2) making humanity nothing more than a mere instrument of the will of God, being acted on rather than acting, and so wholly subject to absolute necessity in all actions. To the first Calvin responds that human nature was not created as evil by God but has become evil by humanity's own disobedience. To the second he affirms that when God acts on someone that person also acts; yet people are so corrupt that their "whole conversion," from beginning to end, must be the gift of God. In other words, God must make a person willing before he or she can will with God.

Pighius had also claimed for himself, and for Augustine, a "middle way" that combines human free choice and God's grace. Calvin responds that Pighius really provided for no "diminution" in human nature as a result of the fall and so was really Pelagian. He also showed by numerous citations that Pighius was wrong about Augustine; Calvin quotes Augustine again to say that he does not know anything good that can be found in the will of fallen humanity.

Furthermore, Pighius had indicated that God should have a reason for bestowing grace on some and not on others. Calvin responds that the answer is not in human ability and lies within the secret will of God. He notes that the goodness of God, to be fully praiseworthy, does not have to be equally accessible to all, and that it "shines better" when God proves it to some and displays his wrath in others. He also cites the Council of Orange to show that Pighius's views were not in accord with its pronouncements.

Book Six (*BLW* 203–44). The final section in Calvin's volume deals with Pighius's arguments and the Scriptures he had used to support his views, versus Calvin's arguments and the Scriptures to which he had appealed. Calvin answers Pighius's arguments in reply to Calvin's arguments in the *Institutes*. For the most part, earlier arguments are repeated and strengthened. He closes with yet another appeal to Augustine, this time to the work entitled *Rebuke and Grace*.

One notes that Calvin's approach to the argument about free will, replying to Pighius, is very different from that of Luther in his reply to Erasmus. As Calvin's editor, A. N. S. Lane, observes, "In many ways it is remarkable how little they have in common" (*BLW* xxvii). Where Luther had insisted (and Erasmus had more or less agreed) that they use only the Scriptures for their arguments, Calvin and Pighius made extensive use of the fathers, with Calvin relying most heavily on Augustine—which must have been a source of frustration to Pighius. Where Luther made much of foreknowledge and the doctrine of absolute necessity, Calvin had much less to say. In contrast to Luther, he never relies on foreknowledge to argue against free will; indeed, I do not think the word appears in his volume. He deals with the doctrine of necessity, to be sure, but it does not have the same prominent role in his work as in Luther's. Interestingly, Calvin makes no reference at all to the earlier debate between Luther and Erasmus. Lane appears to think that Calvin was somewhat embarrassed by some of Luther's observations on the subject but did not want to threaten "Protestant solidarity" by criticizing him (*BLW* xxviii). I leave that for others to judge.

Understanding Calvin

The Concept of Free Will That Calvin Was Resisting

Placing Calvin's arguments in context requires that we know what he was arguing against: namely, the concept of free will that Pighius held. That is easy enough to determine, at least as Calvin understood Pighius, since Calvin frequently quotes or summarizes Pighius's observations. I have selected a few of Calvin's representations of Pighius, showing what he took Pighius's view of free will to mean.

(1) We have the "power" to do what God commands, to do good or evil (*BLW* 24).

(2) One can "prepare himself" to receive God's grace (*BLW* 26).

(3) People are able to "conceive [faith] themselves" (*BLW* 32).

(4) The will is "autonomous" (*BLW* 67–68).

(5) Sin is "avoidable" or else it cannot be accounted as sin (*BLW* 143).

(6) People have the "ability" to move God to give them grace (*BLW* 199–200).

Calvin is arguing against such ideas as these when he emphasizes that man has fallen into such a corrupt condition that he is "unable to arise by his own power" (*BLW* 86). As far as Calvin is concerned, Pighius had affirmed that the fall resulted in no "diminution" in human nature; consequently, Pighius's views are little if any better, and maybe worse, than those of Pelagius (*BLW* 180, 189).

Calvin's Concept of the Human Will

Calvin is careful to maintain that before the fall the first human beings possessed free will. In their original circumstances in Eden, they were not inclined toward sin but could choose good (obedience) or evil (disobedience). As he expresses it, the original couple had a nature that was "entirely pure and perfect" (*BLW* 40). They were innocent, endowed with "uprightness of will" (BLW 46–47). Once they sinned, however, that freedom was lost. Their nature became wholly corrupt and their wills—"spoiled" and "bearing spoiled fruit" (*BLW* 186–87)—were from then on capable of choosing only evil. The power of choice is now free only to do wrong (*BLW* 47–48). Consequently, humanity after the fall does not have free will, at least not in the usual sense of those words.

Calvin is willing to speak of freedom of choice, however, but not if that is understood to mean that a fallen person can freely choose the good. If the words are to be used, they must mean only that the unconverted freely choose evil and that the regenerate choose good only when made willing by God. In both cases, the will is not being forced or coerced, as Calvin sees it, but moves in a "self-determined" agreement with what is acting on it (*BLW* 103). To say this another way, the volition involved in human choices is self-determined (which is the only sense in which it can be called "free"), but even that volition is produced by God when he turns it toward the good (*BLW* 122). In other words, as Augustine expressed it, with Calvin's approval, God "causes" our faith, "working miraculously in our hearts so that we believe" (*BLW* 131).

Only when a person is regenerated by an entirely gracious act of God, when the will is "formed towards obedience" by the work of the Spirit (*BLW* 161), is freedom restored. Even then, there is an important difference, since Adam and Eve had by grace the freedom to choose evil or to choose good— and chose evil. There is a greater grace in regeneration, in that human beings are caused to choose the good (*BLW* 177–78). Adam had grace "to be able not to sin"; the grace given to the regenerate is "not to be able to sin" (*BLW* 240).

Calvin's Reasons for Rejecting Free Will

While my purpose does not include giving attention to every single argument Calvin made against the freedom of the will, I do intend to describe his main reasons for rejecting that concept. These are the grounds out of which all his argument grows. All of them run throughout the work and can be found in many of his discussions.

One: Human depravity. For Calvin, humanity—because of the corruption of its nature that has resulted from original sin and the fall—does not now have free will. For this reason he objects to the use of "free" to modify the (fallen) will, since the word implies an ability within the will itself to choose good or evil (*BLW* 68). In one discussion he compares a paralytic who has lost the ability to walk (*BLW* 97). He insists that the human will is entirely evil, with not "a drop of goodness" (*BLW* 207), and must be transformed by the gracious act of God. This grace, he says, does not merely enable a person to accept or reject the good, but it actually "steers the mind" and "moves the will" to bring about the choice and completion of the good (*BLW* 114). In that choice, the person is "acting" while being "acted upon" (by God), but without the latter the former would not be possible (*BLW* 116).

For Calvin, then, there is no way to overcome this corruption, this bondage of the will, this human inability, except by regeneration. That must come first, and so what is often called "prevenient grace" *is* regeneration. In that regeneration the will is made willing; the very "will to believe" is produced by God's Spirit in this work (*BLW* 119). Even the person's "assent" to God is God's work: we assent, but God works that assent in us. Because of our corruption our assent to God cannot originate with or derive from us (*BLW* 120). He approvingly cites Augustine to say that "it is we who will when we will, but it is he who causes us to will the good" (*BLW* 123, 132).

Two: God's grace as the source of all good. Calvin wanted to be sure that all the credit for humans' salvation, and for anything good done by human beings, is attributed to God's grace and not to anything that issues from them. He agreed with Augustine, who said that after the fall God desired that we "come to him" only by his grace (*BLW* 179). This obviously fits well with the first reason, above, in that corrupt persons cannot even desire God's grace until he has first done a gracious work in them (*BLW* 184).

Calvin strenuously objected to Pighius's suggestion that God gives grace to us only if we first "stretch out our hand" for it (*BLW* 198).

In defending this concept, Calvin acknowledges passages like Isaiah 66:2, which affirms that the Lord shows mercy to those who are humble and contrite, a passage Pighius had cited to show that a person must prepare himself for grace. Calvin insists that it is the Lord's work to make some humble and contrite, that this cannot come about naturally, and that it is the supernatural work of regeneration that brings it about (*BLW* 193). Furthermore, said Calvin, God does not in grace simply make it possible for a person to accept or reject him. Instead, God's grace carries the work through to its end and makes the will good; grace is offered *only* to be effective (*BLW* 195). Where Pighius cited Revelation 3:20, Calvin insists that God is the one who, as a gracious gift, opens the door on which he knocks (*BLW* 197). He acknowledges that God commands us to endeavor to do what is good and to pray, but he insists that we can do so only by his gracious gift (*BLW* 182).

Calvin insists that God shows our goodness to be nothing "by attributing every portion of our good works to himself and his grace" (*BLW* 138). He adds that God desires that his grace be extolled as both generous and free, and that if it is free it must be bestowed only on those whom he chooses to be objects of his grace (*BLW* 200). This means that a person has no role in the choosing except for the choosing God works in that person.

Three: The all-encompassing government of God. Closely related to the first two reasons is this one, although the implications for free will are not quite as direct. Calvin held confidently to the doctrine of providence, meaning that God is "in charge of the world," that he so governs human beings that he "bends their wills this way and that" and they "do nothing which he has not decreed." Thus all things happen necessarily in manifestation of the "eternal and steadfast" purpose of God who is "sovereign in governing them" (*BLW* 38).

All human affairs are included in this. They do not take place by chance but in "the fixed purpose of God" (*BLW* 39) and so by necessity. Calvin was careful, more than once, to distinguish between this *necessity* and *coercion* or *force*. For him, a *coerced* will is one that is "forcibly driven by an external impulse" (*BLW* 69). *Necessity*, on the other hand, means "whatever has to be as it is and cannot be otherwise" (*BLW* 149). He insists that human choices are necessary but not coerced. The evil acts of fallen persons are necessary but entirely self-determined. So are the good choices of the regenerate, even though they are made willing by God. Calvin, at least, sees no contradiction in that; he is quick to say that humans act, even though they act as directed by God (*BLW* 38). He says that the necessity for fallen human beings to act wickedly arises from the corruption of their nature brought on themselves, but he also says that the necessity in wicked acts arises "from the fact that God accomplishes his work . . . through them" (*BLW* 37).

When Pighius accused Calvin and the other Reformers of saying that human beings do not act but are only acted upon, Calvin insisted that people also act as they are acted on by God's grace. Even so, he acknowledges that this works in such a way that the efficacy of the acting is entirely under God's control (*BLW* 172).

Summary: Calvin's View of the Human Will and Salvation

Perhaps a lengthy summary is not necessary, since the main elements of Calvin's view have been indicated above. For him, the issue is not humanity as originally created by God; Adam and Eve had free will. But once they sinned—and all humankind participated with them in that sin and its consequences—the whole mass of the human race has been so corrupted in nature that the will is in bondage and free only to sin—if that is "freedom" at all. In this condition, human beings have no power within themselves to turn to God or even to desire God or his ways.

Consequently, the whole race rests under the condemnation of God, spiritually dead and blind and deaf, unable even to seek to live, much less to unstop its ears or open its eyes. How then can anyone, since our will is wholly given to resist God and cannot be redirected from within, be saved? The answer is that God chose some from that mass of humankind in whom to demonstrate the glory of his grace and determined to demonstrate the glory of his wrath in the rest. Given their implacable rebellion, he can only save them by regenerating them from the inside out. He does not drag them to himself unwillingly, but by regeneration he works willingness within them.

Then they have not chosen to receive grace. Instead, God has chosen them and graciously brought them back to life so that they can and do believe in him. These chosen ones meet no prior condition; they have no choice in the matter. The others, the damned, once having participated in original sin, likewise have no choice except to continue in their sins. Regenerating grace has not been made available to them. Salvation is wholly the work of God, provided and applied unconditionally.

I will, of course, speak to these matters in subsequent chapters. My purpose does not include interacting with Calvin here. I am glad to say, however, that Calvin was right in many things. He was right to emphasize the total inability of fallen people to initiate contact with God. He was right to insist that God has an all-encompassing plan for his world, including humankind, and that he cannot be thwarted in what he has planned. And he was right to set forth salvation as a work of God's grace alone.

6

Jonathan Edwards against Free Will

JONATHAN EDWARDS (1703–1758) IS widely hailed as the greatest American theologian, having "produced one of the most thorough and compelling bodies of theological writing in the history of America."[1] He was the son of a Congregational minister and followed in his father's footsteps. After graduating from Yale he entered the ministry in 1726 and soon began a lengthy pastorate in Northampton, Massachusetts. This ended in 1750 when a controversy about membership requirements resulted in the church dismissing him from office. Afterward he ministered in frontier Stockbridge, Massachusetts, where he preached both to Native Americans and to settlers. He died in 1758, from a smallpox inoculation, shortly after becoming president of the College of New Jersey (now Princeton University).

Edwards is known as the theological voice of the First Great Awakening in America (c. 1745–1753), complementing George Whitfield's preaching. But Edwards was well known for his preaching, too, and some of his sermons may be even more famous than his theological works. His "Sinners in the Hands of an Angry God" (1741), for example, was so powerful that it is still studied as a classic in American literature.

The work with which I am interacting in this volume was first published in 1754 as *A Careful and Strict Enquiry into the Modern Prevailing Notions of That Freedom of Will, Which Is Supposed to Be Essential to Moral Agency, Vertue* [sic] *and Vice, Reward and Punishment, Praise and Blame.* I will use the more recent Yale University Press edition (cited in the text as *FW*). Unlike Luther and Calvin, Edwards did not write in response to a

---

1. Noll, *Evangelical Dictionary of Theology*, 343. This is a helpful article on Edwards and his contributions to theology, and my brief summary here depends heavily on it.

specific volume attacking free will. Even so, he wrote in opposition to some fairly well-known spokesmen against the Calvinism he espoused. Three in particular he referred to frequently throughout his treatise on the subject: Thomas Chubb, Daniel Whitby, and Isaac Watts—all Englishmen.[2]

Chubb (1679–1747) earned his living in secular pursuits but spent a large part of his time writing theological tracts. His theology, however, was not well fixed: he began as an Arian and moved on to support Deism, a school of thought in which the freedom of the will was strongly emphasized.

Whitby (1638–1726) was a minister in the Church of England whose first writings were against Roman Catholicism. When he began urging tolerance for dissenters from the Church of England, he met with opposition and some of his books were burned. During the time of his ministry the Church of England was loosely Arminian in tendency, and Whitby published his *Discourse on the Five Points* in 1710 to oppose a Calvinist minister in the Church. This is the treatise Edwards cited in his work. The later work of Whitby, published after his death as he directed, showed Arian and Unitarian tendencies.

Watts (1674–1748), sometimes classified as an "uneasy Calvinist," was a Nonconformist minister but is better known as a composer of widely loved hymns, many of them still sung in Christian churches in various denominations. His tendencies were toward reconciling those of different persuasions, including Arminians and Calvinists, Arians and Trinitarians, and the dissenting Independents and Baptists. In this last effort he proposed, for example, that the Independents give up infant baptism and that the Baptists give up immersion.[3] He was sometimes accused of Arian tendencies. Edwards responded to his *An Essay on Freedom of Will in God and in Creatures*, published in 1732.

What is clear from this brief summary is that, in fact, Edwards's opponents—like Erasmus and Pighius, whom Luther and Calvin targeted—were not evangelical Arminians. Even so, it seems clear that many of Edwards's arguments against free will might well have been the same had he crossed swords, say, with Arminius himself or with the English General Baptist theologian Thomas Grantham (1634–1692) or the Wesleyan Richard Watson (1781–1833). His work is too influential for us not to take seriously.

---

2. See Ramsey, *Jonathan Edwards Freedom of the Will*, 65–118, in his section "Edwards and His Antagonists" for a longer, helpful description of these men and Edwards's interaction with them. My brief description is based on this.

3. Ibid., 91.

Edwards against Free Will: An Overview

As in the two preceding chapters on Luther and Calvin, my purpose here does not include a detailed description of Edwards's argument against free will. I do intend to provide, however, a fairly thorough overview, so that the reader can understand his approach and the nature of his reasoning.

His treatise consists of a short preface, four main parts, and a conclusion. In Part One, he deals with the terms and definitions involved in the discussion of free will. In order, he discusses (1) the nature of the will, (2) what it means to "determine" the will, (3) the meaning of terms like *necessity* and *contingency*, (4) the difference between natural and moral necessity, and (5) the meaning of liberty and moral agency. The will is a "faculty or power or principle of mind by which it is capable of choosing" (*FW* 137). To "determine" the will is, in consequence of some action or influence, to *cause* the choice it makes (*FW* 141).

For Edwards, *necessity* means that there is an infallible (certain) connection between an event, including human volition, and anything antecedent to it which is the ground or reason for its being what it is. Opposite to this is *contingency*, something which comes to pass without any connection to a cause or antecedent and thus "has absolutely no previous ground or reason" (*FW* 155). There are two kinds of necessity. Natural necessity involves the force of natural law and prevails without regard to the will. Moral necessity, however, involves the will and is in effect when a person's biases, inclinations, or motives are so strong that the choice made cannot be otherwise. This is the "necessity" Edwards defends. Liberty, then, means simply the ability to choose *as one pleases*—even though moral necessity means that what the person pleases can only be what it is. So long as the person is not forced against his will, he is at liberty and so is a moral agent and responsible.

In Part Two (the lengthiest part of the book) Edwards considers whether there can be any such thing as what Arminians mean by "free will," making a number of logical arguments against what he understands to be their concept. The first of these is of central importance in the case he makes and undergirds all the rest. Arminians, he says, define free will to mean the power of "self-determination." Seizing on that word, Edwards defines it to mean that the self "determines its own acts by choosing its own acts." He then interprets this to require an act of the will that determines the act of the will, so that every free act of choice is preceded by another free act of choice. This, he says, must either lead us back to infinite regress (my wording) or to an initial act of choice that was *not* free, which would then mean that none of the acts in the chain were free. Either way, the idea that acts of the will are "self-determined" is "absurd" (*FW* 172).

Edwards anticipates that Arminians may claim they do not mean that one act of the will precedes and determines another act of the will, but only that the soul "determines its own volitions." He pronounces this an "evasion" and ridicules it with his own arguments that assume cause-effect relationships (*FW* 175–76). He insists that Arminians hold that the will "influences, orders and determines itself" to act in making a choice, which requires a choice that causes a choice, even though Arminians think choices are uncaused and contingent (*FW* 178–79).

The rest of Part Two builds on this. Edwards argues (§3) that all events, including volitions, are the effects of "causes," defining this word broadly: a *cause* is any antecedent that is connected to an event in such a way that it is "the ground or reason" of the event, even if it exerts no positive influence and is "perhaps rather an occasion than a cause, most properly speaking" (*FW* 180–81). In fine rationalistic form he affirms that anything not self-existent (and so eternal) must begin to be, and anything that begins to be must have a cause; otherwise, we have no way of knowing anything, including the existence of God. He ridicules the idea of Watts (§4) that spirits can originate ideas without causes and proceeds to reiterate (§5) that the Arminian notion requires a free choice going before the free act of the will, which results either in infinite regress or the contradiction of a first choice caused by a prior choice (*FW* 192).

Edwards offers other objections. Arminians, he says, require that a free will act in *indifference* (§6), which illogically implies that one exercises preference without having a preference (*FW* 196). Pressing this point (§7), he insists that this would require *absolute* freedom from all prior inclinations, which is not possible, and that when a will is already inclined it is bound and cannot act except as it is inclined (*FW* 205). Furthermore, Arminians require that the will be free from *necessity* so as to act contingently (§8), but all events are necessarily connected with their antecedent causes and there is no such contingency as Arminians require (*FW* 215–16). This "connection" applies equally to the dictates of a person's *understanding* (§9) and *motives* (§10), which would again lead the Arminian into a contradiction, since these are causes and mean that the will acts out of necessity.

Edwards proceeds, then, to argue his case from *foreknowledge*. After proving from Scripture that God has exhaustive foreknowledge (§11), he provides a logical demonstration that God's foreknowledge is necessary and so the things infallibly foreknown by him (including human volitions) are equally necessary. He concludes this part by insisting (§13) that Arminians must either acknowledge necessity in acts of the will or be left with nothing but randomness and chance—since the opposite of necessity is contingency and contingency means not being caused.

In Part Three of the work, Edwards considers whether, as Arminians contend, the kind of free will they insist on is essential to moral agency—to virtue and vice, or to praise and blame. His conclusion is, of course, that it is not. For one thing, God himself is *necessarily* good and yet is certainly praiseworthy for that (§1). Likewise (§2), the acts of the will of Jesus Christ, considered from the perspective of his human nature, were *necessarily* holy, and yet his behavior was praiseworthy. Furthermore, those whom God has "given up" to sin must at least from that point on sin *necessarily*, and even so they are blameworthy (§3). There is therefore no logical contradiction between necessary behavior and the kind of responsibility required of a moral agent or deserving of praise and blame.

Furthermore, the fact that God commands obedience is not, as Arminians say, inconsistent with moral inability (§4). So-called sincere desires and efforts, as may be found in the natural human being but fall short of genuine repentance, are not really virtuous at all and so do not excuse the person (§5). Indeed, the Arminians' "liberty of indifference" is not only unnecessary to true virtue but inconsistent with it (§6), since being morally indifferent is certainly not virtuous but is instead wicked. Indeed, any habitual tendency toward good or evil, which everyone acknowledges as praise- or blame-worthy, would violate that indifference. For that matter, any use of motives and inducements to good or evil would also destroy the Arminian "indifference" (§7).

Edwards devotes Part Four, primarily, to countering the main arguments of Arminians. He argues that Arminians find virtue and vice in the *cause* of their acts—i.e., in being self-determined—whereas it is really in the *nature* of those acts (§1). He attacks the Arminians' "metaphysical" notions of action and agency (§2): they require that the action of an agent be uncaused, and yet they hold that one's action is the effect of its own determination. He attempts to explain why Arminians have fallen into incorrect belief (§3), blaming it on the habitual use of terms, and proceeds to distinguish natural necessity (which he agrees would be contrary to agency and to praise- and blame-worthiness) from moral necessity (which he insists is not contrary to that). Indeed, he affirms, moral necessity is fully agreeable to common sense (§4).

Edwards then proceeds to answer Arminian objections that if humans act entirely by necessity, all means and efforts toward good are in vain and people are mere machines (§5). He observes that such means are part of the chain of connected events, and that includes the reason and understanding of human beings that makes them fundamentally different from machines. Furthermore, Calvinistic doctrine is *not* in agreement with the fatalistic doctrine of the Stoics or the opinions of Hobbes (§6). And Watts was incorrect in denying that God himself acts by necessity (§7, §8).

At length, Edwards responds to the argument that Calvinism makes God the author of sin (§9). God is not a sinner, nor the agent, actor, or doer of sin, but he is the permitter—or not the hinderer—of sin. He "disposes" all events in such a way that sin "will most certainly and infallibly follow," but he does so for his own "wise, holy and most excellent ends and purposes" (*FW* 399), and only in that sense is he the "author" of sin—although Edwards does not prefer that wording. God may "in his providence so dispose and permit things" that will certainly and infallibly be connected to evil without himself being guilty of any evil (*FW* 406).

Edwards then proceeds to discuss the entrance of the first sin into the world (§10): God, when he created man, so ordered "his circumstances, that from these circumstances, together with his [God's] withholding further assistance and divine influence, his sin would infallibly follow" (*FW* 413). If these things appear to be inconsistent with God's moral character and benevolent will, one must distinguish between God's "perceptive" and his "disposing" will (§11). The first expresses what God loves, as in his counsels and invitations; the second expresses "what he chooses as a part of his own infinite scheme of things" (*FW* 415). Arminians who acknowledge the exhaustive foreknowledge of God are, in fact, no better off. Furthermore, these principles do not lead to atheism or licentiousness, as some Arminians affirm (§12). Indeed, the Arminians' insistence that choices arise without any connection to or dependence on anything foregoing—and so are uncaused and without any ground or reason—is what really leads to atheism (*FW* 420).

Finally, Edwards responds to the charge that such reasoning as his is too metaphysical and abstract (§13). If it is, that does not make it wrong; but in fact it is not. At this point Edwards more or less sums up the argument of his book in order to insist that it is not abstruse, and a lengthy quotation seems justified to assist the reader in grasping the whole.

There is no high degree of refinement and abstruse speculation, in determining, that a thing is not before it is, and so can't be the cause of itself; or that the first act of free choice, has not another act of free choice going before that, to excite or direct it; or in determining, that no choice is made, while the mind remains in a state of absolute indifference; that preference and equilibrium never coexist; and that therefore no choice is made in a state of liberty, consisting in indifference; and that so far as the will is determined by motives, exhibited and operating previous to itself; that nothing can begin to be, which before was not, without a cause, or some antecedent ground or reason, why it then begins to be; that effects depend on their causes, and are connected with them; that virtue· is not the worse, nor sin the better, for the strength of inclination, with which it is practiced, and the difficulty which thence arises of doing otherwise; that when it is already infallibly known, that a thing will be, it is not a thing contingent whether it will ever be or no; or that it can be truly said, notwithstanding, that it is not necessary it should be, but it either may be, or may not be. And the like might be observed of many other things which belong to the foregoing reasoning. (*FW* 424–25)

In his Conclusion, Edwards links his treatment of free will to the basic teachings of Calvinism, indicating that what he has said on the subject is thoroughly coherent with those teachings. These teachings include God's all-inclusive, determining providence; human total depravity; God's efficacious and irresistible grace; God's absolute and universal decrees, including election; Christ's particular atonement; and the doctrine of the infallible and necessary perseverance of the saints. It is important to note, however, that the work itself does not use any of these doctrines as a basis for its treatment of free will.

Understanding Edwards

The Method of Edwards

Unlike Luther and Calvin, who argued their case in biblical and theological categories, Edwards, for whatever reasons—perhaps to supplement the standard treatments—chose rationalistic method. To understand him, then, one must reckon with this.

There is more than one way to make an argument or pursue truth. At least three methods are widely touted, grounded respectively (primarily, but not exclusively) in three sources: reason, experience, and divine revelation. At risk of oversimplification, I will describe each of these briefly, taking them in reverse order.

The third is the method of biblical exegesis, in attempting to ascertain (using linguistic and historical resources) what the text actually says, what implications can certainly be drawn from the text, and how to express the information in a systematic way. This is the usual method of Christian theology. Somewhat surprisingly, it is not the method of Edwards, even though in a few places that is his approach, notably in Part Two, Section 11, where he proves God's exhaustive foreknowledge. This method, of course, is not useful for philosophy, which relies on one or both of the other methods.

The second, empirical method, is the method of modern science. It lends itself well to the quest for knowledge of the physical universe. By this method one seeks to make as many observations of physical evidence as possible, then from those observations to construct a hypothesis that would explain the observations, then to test and refine the hypothesis on the basis of further experimental observations, and to continue this process until virtual certainty is obtained. This is a good method, but its effectiveness is by definition limited to those aspects of our world and experience that can be observed by the senses. This also, although it is the method preferred by some philosophers (David Hume is often regarded as representative), is not the method of Edwards.

The rationalistic method, the first of the three, seeks for indisputable ("self-evident") truths and then attempts to draw out whatever is necessarily and logically implied by them. Philosophers regard René Descartes, for example, as a quintessential rationalist. He thought he discovered a first truth in "I think, therefore I am"[4] and believed he could rationally demonstrate not only his own existence but also that of God and the physical world from that starting point. The degree of his success is still debated, and to enter that debate is not within my purpose here. I simply want the reader to understand that this is the method of Edwards. His editor, Paul Ramsey, observes that much of the book consists "wholly of philosophical clarification and reasoning," and that he "returns again and again to philosophical analysis."[5]

Empirical method tends to rely heavily on *a posteriori* ("from what follows") reasoning, from particular observations to the general operations that lie behind and explain them: from effect to cause, in other words.

---

4. *Cogito ergo sum.*

5. Ramsey, *Jonathan Edwards Freedom of the Will*, 9.

Rationalistic method, by contrast, tends to rely on *a priori* ("from what pre-cedes") reasoning, from general truths to particular implications of those truths: from cause to effect, in other words.

The rationalistic method emphasizes cause-effect relationships and the logical relations between them. It is the method often used, for example, by evidentialist apologists who argue from first causes, as in the cosmologi-cal argument for the existence of God. Norman Geisler, a contemporary apologist, bases his argument on such reasoning: everything that exists must be either necessary or contingent, and every contingent thing must be traceable back to a necessary Being. Given the fact that nothing in our cosmos *has* to exist, it must have been given existence by a Being that *has* to. Consequently, there must be a God who created the universe, the Un-caused First Cause.[6]

Edwards grounds an important part of his reasoning on this very sort of argument.

> What is self-existent must be from eternity, and must be unchange-able: but as to all things that *begin to be*, they are not self-existent, and therefore must have some foundation of their existence with-out themselves. That whatsoever begins to be, which before was not, must have a cause why it then begins to exist, seems to be the first dictate of the common and natural sense which God hath implanted in the minds of all mankind, and the main foundation of all our reasonings about the existence of things, past, present, or to come. (*FW* 181)

Thus he indicates his heavy reliance on the several aspects of the rationalistic method: self-evident truths, first causes, and cause-effect relationships as logi-cally compelling. This is, I think, what Allen Guelzo means when he observes that the arguments of *Freedom of the Will* are "predicated on a risky series of analytic propositions about the terms and processes of human volition."[7] Knowing that Edwards included human volitions—acts of the will—among "things that *begin to be*" and therefore in the category of effects of causes goes a long way to understanding his argument against freedom of the will.

The rationalistic method, making use as it does of logical proofs, tends to rely on *analysis* of an opponent's propositions, breaking them down so as

6. This is, of course, a dreadful over-simplification of Geisler's highly refined argu-ment; see his *Christian Apologetics*. His article "Freedom, Free Will, and Determinism," in Elwell, *Evangelical Dictionary of Theology*, 428–30, will help the reader understand both the method and Edwards's use of it.

7. Guelzo, "Jonathan Edwards and the Possibilities of Free Will," 90.

to be able to show that they are logically "self-defeating." I am not suggesting that there is anything wrong with this kind of argumentation. (I have used it, for example, against secular empiricists who emphatically affirm that there is no knowledge apart from what is learned by empirical method—when, in fact, that very affirmation, which is obviously a claim to know something, is *not* learned by empirical method!) But whether this kind of argument is convincing to others is a matter of opinion. Those who already agree with one's position will say so, but those who do not may not find it compelling.

Another of Edwards's key arguments grows out of just such analysis. Seizing on the Arminian insistence that volitions depend on *self-determination*, he insists that this requires that one act of the will (the determining) precede another (the free act), and that this leads either to infinite regress or to the contradiction of a *first* choice which is preceded by another and so is not "first" (*FW* 176). This is the rationalistic method in pure form, and Edwards refers back to the same analysis, as a problem for Arminianism, at least a dozen times in the work. (I will have more to say about how this is involved in Edwards's main arguments below.)

The Concept of Free Will Edwards Opposed

As with Luther and Calvin, it is important to discern exactly what view of free will was held by the "Arminians" that Edwards responded to. Unlike those two Reformers, who were resisting the free will of the Roman Catholicism of Erasmus and Pighius, Edwards wrote against the free will of Anglicans and Dissenters in England in the eighteenth century, people who (as noted above) flirted with Arian and Deistic heresy, at that.

But names do not necessarily identify concepts, and Edwards reveals just what concepts were held by those he disagreed with, whom he calls "Arminians." The key elements of their view are indicated in many of Edwards's observations, not counting the places where he says what he thinks Arminian views must imply.

In summary, Edwards's Arminians held three main concepts, to which he returns often, as follows. First, they held that real "liberty" is grounded in *self-determination*, meaning that volitions, or acts of the will, cannot be dependent on any cause outside the self or on anything prior to those acts. Second, they held that a will, to be free, must act from *indifference*, which Edwards took to mean that the mind is in a state of equilibrium before volition, that is, not already inclined one way or the other. Third, they held that whatever is done freely requires *contingency*, as opposed to necessity or to "any fixed and certain connection with some previous ground or reason of its existence" (*FW* 164–65).

Some additional observations by Edwards serve to add detail. He says Arminians required, in their view of free will, that "the determination of volition is without a cause" and that "the free acts of the will are contingent events" (*FW* 179) and are not done by necessity (*FW* 192). This meant, according to Edwards, that the Arminian view included contingency as the opposite of constraint or of a consequence where one thing infallibly follows from another (*FW* 213).

Edwards further attributes to Arminians the idea that if an act is made necessary—that is, caused—by something outside the self, the act has no moral value; only if caused by something within the self is the person blame- or praise-worthy (*FW* 338). Likewise, any "action" that is necessitated by the action of another is not an action and the doer is not an agent: "necessary agent" is a contradiction (*FW* 343). What is "necessary" is "inconsistent with virtue and vice, praise and blame, reward and punishment"—and Edwards observes that in saying this the Arminians make "no distinction between natural and moral necessity" (*FW* 350).

Edwards's Concept of the Will

The basic element of Edwards's concept of the human will is that it is at liberty ("free") to choose as it pleases: in other words, in accord with its own desires. To exercise the will is the same as to choose (*FW* 137), and a person never "wills anything contrary to his desires, or desires anything contrary to his will" (*FW* 139). This means that fallen human beings are at liberty only to sin, but one has to know that Edwards was a committed Calvinist to realize this; unlike Calvin and Luther, he does not take pains to indicate so.

If this explains how fallen human beings are free only to choose evil, it does not explain how the original parents became sinners. As noted above (see *FW* 413–14), Edwards affirms that God placed them in circumstances where their choice of sin was necessary, although he did so for a holy purpose, apparently knowing that a world where evil exists is better than one where it does not. He has so ordered things that, by his permitting, "sin will come to pass; for the sake of the great good that by his disposal shall be the consequence" (*FW* 408–9).

Equally important to Edwards's concept of the will is that all its voli-tions are caused. A volition is an "existent" (that which exists) and yet it is not self-existent. Anything that begins to exist (and so did not always exist) must have a cause outside itself to account for its existence. Cause-effect relations apply to everything except God himself. The volitions of persons are not exceptions. True, a cause is not necessarily a mechanical force like that which exists between a strike of lightning and the peal of thunder that follows, but the mental understandings antecedent to volitions are their causes. Such understandings are formed by various kinds of influences, including appeals, motivations, warnings, and the like. The connection between these and the choice made by the person is an infallible one and therefore qualifies as a cause-effect relationship. A person always chooses whatever makes the strongest appeal to his mind. Choices infallibly follow from prevailing motivations and inclinations, from what "appears most agreeable and pleasing, all things considered" (FW 147).

Edwards means the same thing as this when he says that all volitions, like all events, are necessary. He distinguishes between natural and moral necessity. The first is seen, primarily, with the operation of natural law, "through the force of natural causes," as when a person is wounded he feels pain. This is not the kind of necessity Edwards presents as operating on the will. Instead, it is *moral* necessity, which is in effect when a person's under-standing or biases or inclinations or motivations are strong enough that they inevitably lead to the choice made, when there is a "perfect connec-tion between moral causes and effects" (FW 156–57). The same distinction applies to *inability*: natural inability is in effect when we are unable to do something even if we will it because natural law is against it; moral inability consists in the absence of an inclination or one strong enough, or "of suf-ficient motives, to induce and excite the act of the will to the contrary" (FW 159). Significantly, and in accord with what I have said above about the freedom to do as one pleases, Edwards adds that "a man can't be truly said to be unable to do a thing, when he can do it if he will"; indeed, "the very willing is the doing" (FW 162).

One sees, then, that Edwards's concept of the human will and its "free-dom" is in accord with a view called *compatibilism*, although he does not use the term itself—which was not available to him, having been coined, apparently, in the twentieth century. I have defined this worldview in another chapter. It is enough to say here that campatibilists believe that one can hold to determinism and freedom at the same time without being logically incoherent. They say that freedom of will does not require being able to make either of two contrary choices, only that one is free to act in accord with the sum total of all the circumstances, including his mental and emotional states, bearing on him at the time of choice. This is the view of the will and its freedom that Edwards held.

Edwards's Reasons for Rejecting Free Will

By now, the arguments Edwards lodged against the Arminian concept of free will have already been made clear. To avoid extensive repetition, then, I will do little more than to list and comment briefly on his main objections. The discussion given above will point the reader to elucidation of these arguments.

I should add, lest the reader has missed this, that in this volume Edwards does not argue on the basis of traditional Calvinistic theology. His approach is that of a rationalistic philosopher, not a theologian. Perhaps he felt that the theological treatments in existence were sufficient and that a philosophical approach would strengthen the case, but he does not say that. It is clear, however, that his Calvinistic theology provided the fundamental assumptions that grounded his views, and his Conclusion makes this clear.

In this volume, then, Edward's main reasons for denying free will, as popularly conceived, are these three, closely interwoven.

One: The law of cause and effect. As I have already indicated, Edwards relied heavily on cause-effect relationships in his resistance to free will. In the same way that some apologists think to prove the existence of God as first cause, so he argued that human choices must also have causes. Our volitions have not always existed and so begin their existence at some point. They are therefore not *self-existent*, else they would be eternal; and this seems to be at least a part of his reason for ridiculing the idea of *self-determination*. Anything that is not self-existent has to have a cause for its existence other than itself, and that applies to human volitions as well as humans themselves.

Human choices, then, cannot arise willy-nilly, as it were, out of thin air. Lying behind them are various circumstances deriving from information, understanding, motivations, inclinations, influences, passions, desires, and the like. These are the causes of the volitions. In fact, they make the specific choices certain to be what they are, so certain that they cannot be otherwise. Cause-effect relationships are just as real in acts of the will as the forces that make one's automobile run—although not of the same nature.

Two: All-inclusive necessity. Closely related to his insistence on cause-effect explanations for the existence of volitions and all other events is Edwards's concept of necessity as prevailing in all actions in the world. For Edwards, this can be seen from either of two different perspectives, but both lead to the same unerring conclusion that everything that takes place does so by necessity.

One perspective is found in what has just been said about cause and effect. Every effect—and that includes human volition—has before it a cause that renders it infallible and necessary. The other perspective is found in divine foreknowledge. Whatever God knows will come to pass, and he knows the future exhaustively; therefore it cannot but come to pass. That, too, indicates necessity.

As has been noted, Edwards distinguishes between two kinds of necessity, physical (involving the working of natural law) and moral (involving the activity of moral agents), and it is the latter that is in effect in acts of the will. Nonetheless, they are just as necessary, although of a somewhat different nature, as things that must be what they are because of natural law.

But Edwards introduces into his discussion of necessity some admissions that tend to confuse the issue. This he does by equating necessity with (mere) *certainty*, and the equating of the two terms allows one to think that he may not be saying, after all, what he appears to be saying. I will return to this matter in chapter 7, on foreknowledge and necessity.

Three: The logical absurdity of self-determination. Again, this is closely related to the preceding two reasons, although both of them seem more fundamental. At any rate, Edwards seizes on the term *self-determination* and never tires of attacking it as logically self-contradictory or of ridiculing it as absurd.

Do the Arminians insist that acts of the will are "self-determined"? What can this mean but that there is a self behind every choice, determining the choice? And this means that the act of determining precedes the choice! But for that act of determining to be self-determined there would then have to be yet another volition before it and determining it. And this leads to infinite regress, which all logicians know is a dead end.

If that infinite regress is to be avoided, one must go back to a *first* choice of some sort, one that started the whole chain of choices. Then one faces a dilemma. If that first choice is uncaused, then it arises out of nothing, without any explanation or reason for its existence, and that is impossible. If, however, it is caused, then one is left with the self-contradictory notion of a *first* cause that was itself caused by a prior cause, and that of course cannot be.

One probably cannot underestimate the importance of this reasoning in Edwards's case against free will. From the early stages of his work (*FW* 171–74) to near the end (359) and many times in between (192, 219–20, 228–29, 234–35, and others) this argument is reflected. I will return to this matter in the chapter on free will and the logic of cause and effect.

My purpose does not include interaction with Edwards here. As just noted, a subsequent chapter will focus on his logical analysis in particular. He agreed, of course, with Luther and Calvin on the theology of salvation, including fallen humanity's total depravity as rendering people absolutely unable to turn to God in their own ability, God's all-inclusive government of the universe in accord with his eternal and unconditional plan, and that salvation must be entirely a work of God's grace to which humans can contribute nothing that saves them. And in these things he was right. He also agreed that these things mean that fallen humanity does not have free will, a matter I will explore in all the rest of this work.

Even so, Edwards's approach was different from that of Luther and Calvin. He argued against free will on the basis of rationalistic logic. I will speak to that in a chapter devoted entirely to his treatment of the subject. Even so, his logical argument relied heavily on the doctrine of foreknowledge, and so I will also deal with his views in chapter 7, on free will, foreknowledge, and necessity.

Part Three

The Major Issues

7

Free Will, Foreknowledge, and Necessity

CHRISTIAN THEOLOGY TRADITIONALLY MAINTAINS that God knows the future perfectly, and this has sometimes seemed to block human freedom, when that freedom is understood to mean the ability to choose contrary to the way one chooses. The argument is simple and apparently obvious: if God knows that a certain choice will be made, then it is certain that such a choice will be made and nothing different from that is possible. No sophistication is required to follow that logic.

For this reason, some thinkers have denied God's foreknowledge of some things, especially of the free choices of human beings or at least of their *sinful* choices. This "way out" of the apparent, logical contradiction between foreknowledge and freedom lies behind the recent movement that has come to be called "open theism," an innovative and neo-Arminian approach developed by Clark Pinnock, John Sanders, Greg Boyd, and others. My purpose in this chapter does not include responding to that ultimately unorthodox revision of Christian theism. I have done this elsewhere.[1]

I am satisfied that to deny God's exhaustive foreknowledge is clearly unbiblical, and I accept—with Luther, Calvin, and Edwards—that he knows every aspect of the future minutely and infallibly, including the moral choices made by human beings. How, then, can this be reconciled with human freedom? Perhaps it cannot: both Luther and Edwards used the doctrine of foreknowledge in their volumes against free will. (Calvin did not, as I have noted in the chapter devoted to his volume.)

---

1. Picirilli, "Arminian Response to John Sanders," 467–91; "Foreknowledge, Freedom, and the Future," 259–71.

Luther and Foreknowledge

Using foreknowledge to argue against freedom shows up several times in Luther's argument with Erasmus. In one lengthy discussion he makes a number of telling observations, insisting that if God had foreknowledge of Judas's betraying of Jesus, then Judas acted of necessity and "it was not in the power of Judas or of any creature to act differently" (*BW* 213). He buttressed this with the assertion that since God cannot be in error, "then what He foreknows must necessarily come to pass" (*BW* 213). He asserts that to hold to both God's foreknowledge and humanity's freedom would be the same as "maintaining that contraries and contradictories do not clash" (*BW* 215). He offers that God would be "a ludicrous Deity—idol, rather—if his foreknowledge of the future were unreliable and could be falsified by events" (*BW* 216). For Luther, once we acknowledge the foreknowledge and omnipotence of God, it follows that all we do is by necessity (*BW* 218).

In another passage Luther responds to Erasmus's insistence that Judas, even after his coming betrayal was known to Jesus, could have changed his will. How could he have done so, Luther retorts, "while God's infallible foreknowledge stands?" (*BW* 220). He calls this "the central issue in our debate" (*BW* 221) and insists that if his view is not true "God will be mistaken in His foreknowledge . . . and that is impossible" (*BW* 222). "This means that 'free-will' does not exist" (*BW* 222).

I would be remiss if I did not clarify that for Luther this is not merely the *logic* of foreknowledge. Instead, this is grounded in God's foreordination of all things. That he foreknows things and that he foreordains things are inextricably bound together. Thus, for God's foreknowledge to be wrong, his sovereign government of the world must also fail. He notes that "God foreknows nothing contingently, but that He foresees, purposes, and does all things according to His own immutable, eternal and infallible will" and calls this a "bombshell" that "utterly shatters" free will (*BW* 80). Everything we do, then, is "according to what God foreknew and works by His infallible and immutable counsel and power" (*BW* 218).

Edwards and Foreknowledge

Edwards would agree with Luther, no doubt, but he does not make so much out of linking foreknowledge to foreordination, probably because (as I have noted in the chapter on Edwards) he chooses a rationalistic rather than a theological approach. But the argument from foreknowledge is no less strong. Indeed, he devotes two sections (§11 and §12) in Part Two to this matter. In the first he shows from Scripture that God certainly foreknows the volitions (acts of will) of human beings. In the second he argues that this eliminates the possibility of free will as understood by Arminians.

His argument goes this way. God foreknows all things by necessity, and that knowledge is therefore a necessary "existent" (= something that exists). Then the things foreknown, being indissolubly connected with the foreknowledge, must likewise be necessary existents. They cannot therefore be contingent existents, since anything contingent may or may not exist and therefore could not be certainly foreknown. To suppose that God certainly foreknows something uncertain is a contradiction and impossible. Thus Arminians who agree that God certainly foreknows all future events must agree that all events are necessary and not contingent, and this eliminates free will and establishes the necessity of all things (FW 257–69).

Responding to the Argument from Foreknowledge

It remains, then, to answer these two powerful voices. If they are right, the fact of God's foreknowledge cancels the possibility of libertarian free will. But they are not right.

I will answer, here, only that part of the argument that both men shared in common: namely, that foreknowledge *as certain knowledge* of the future, in and of itself makes it logically and really impossible for a person to make any choice other than the one God knows he will make. Unlike Edwards, Luther added to this the element of foreordination; I will respond to that aspect of Luther's objection to free will in chapter 9, on the sovereignty and providence of God.

The Terms Involved

It will be obvious to anyone reading Luther or Edwards that there are some terms that almost control the debate. These terms are *necessity, contingency,* and *certainty.* Any discussion of the issue must proceed on the basis of clear definitions of these terms, definitions that those involved in the discussion must agree to. And the problem is that both Luther and Edwards use the terms without doing this carefully enough. At times, then, some ambiguity creeps into their discussion.

Let me begin by providing definitions that I think will be helpful in understanding the real issues involved.[2] The reader will at least know how I am using the terms. Furthermore, I believe that any discussion of the issues can be advanced if all participants will agree either to use these terms this way or to provide another set of terms that will include words with these agreed-upon meanings. (I am not saying, of course, that these are the only possible ways the words can be used. Words are not like that. I am saying that the meanings I am assigning to these words, for the sake of the discussion of free will, are meanings that must be included in the discussion and that must be assigned to some words by agreement of all.)

Necessity (as it relates to human volitions) I will define as any force or set of circumstances that make only one choice possible. I can see that the word might possibly be used with other nuances of meaning, but we have to have a word that can mean this, and *necessity* (with its cognate words like *necessary, necessitate,* etc.) is the best choice. I believe it is the meaning that most people, without deliberately trying to do otherwise, will assign to necessity, at least when discussing free will. (Using words with philosophical meanings that only the initiated can grasp is not a good idea in discussing things that matter to the faith of the church.) As an example of necessity affecting volitions, I might cite the case of a prisoner, who is necessarily limited in the decisions he can make about his movements.

In other words, a *necessity* is anything that has to be the way it is for any reason other than an act of the will. That reason might be divine action, for example. If, indeed, God hardened Pharaoh's heart arbitrarily, making it impossible from the very beginning for him to do anything other than to refuse to let Israel go, then Pharaoh acted out of necessity. Or the reason might be natural law. Anyone who steps off the top floor of a tall building will of necessity fall—but that has little if anything to do with the exercise of free will in moral decisions or for salvation.

Contingency, on the other hand, I define as any volition that does not have to be what it is, any choice that can go in more than one way. Some theologians will deny that there is any such thing, then, and perhaps all three of those I am responding to would be among them. Even so, there needs to be a word that means this so that the concept can be named and discussed.

Thus *contingency* is the opposite of *necessity,* at least when applied to human volitions. If I say that a choice is contingent, I simply mean that there is nothing outside the self that makes it necessary; some other choice

2. Again I refer the reader to my articles referenced above.

really could be made—and *really* simply means that it could be made in the real world.

That brings us to *certainty*, which I define as anything that was, is, or will be. *Certainty* is nothing more than another way of referring to the *factness* (if I may coin a word) of anything. Everything that has transpired in the past, including human volitions, *certainly* transpired. And everything that will transpire in the future, including human volitions, *certainly* will transpire. In other words, every event in the past, present, or future, including any act of the will, is *certain*.

One should realize that to speak of the certainty of anything is to speak of it as it is. The opposite of a certain future is not an uncertain future: it is no future at all. Every future that will be is certain. Our Spanish-speaking friends have a saying that is often used in a misleading way: *Que sera, sera*, "What will be, will be." It sounds fatalistic, but in fact it says only that what is in the future is in the future. I may say, correctly, that it is *certainly* in the future, but I have not thereby added anything at all to the saying.

Every act of the will is certain, then. It can be certain and contingent. It can be certain and necessary. But it cannot be both contingent and necessary. Those two words cancel each other out; they are opposites. But certainty can go with either of them. Indeed, every necessary event is certain, but so is every contingent event. Where two or more possibilities for the future really exist (if, indeed they do), the one that will be is the one that will be. (Which is to say nothing more significant than to say that a brown cow is a brown cow!)

There are other words that crop up often in the discussion of free will that add more heat than light, words like *possible* and *can* or their negative forms. They are especially elusive and subject to ambiguity. If you ask whether it is *possible* for a person to make, or *can* make, either of two choices, I can answer either way. In one sense, of course, he *cannot* do other than what he will do; in another, he *can*. One speaks of certainty, the other of contingency. It is best, generally, to avoid these terms in the discussion, at least when arguing over them.

Certainty, then, speaks of the facticity of an event: *whether* it will be or not. *Contingency* and *necessity* speak of something else: *how* or *why* something is. We would never say that an event happens "by certainty," but it makes perfect sense to say "by necessity" or "by contingency." A necessary event occurs as a result of circumstances that can yield no alternative choice; a contingent one—we may call it a *conditional* event—occurs as a result of a choice between alternatives.

Luther's and Edwards's Use of the Terms

Luther uses *necessity* from the beginning to the end of his volume, resisting Erasmus's insistence that if human volitions are by necessity then we are not really responsible for them. He takes pains to distinguish between necessity and compulsion or force and insists that by the term *necessity* he means the same thing as *immutability* (*BW* 81, 83–84, 102, 181, 258–59, etc.), which I am left to define as meaning what cannot be changed or otherwise than it is. I have already cited, above, his use of Judas's betrayal of Jesus as an example of this (*BW* 213).

Calvin, likewise, uses *necessity* frequently and distinguishes it from coercion (*BLW* 69, 101, 146–50). But he grounds necessity in God's foreordination and in humanity's depravity rather than in foreknowledge, and so I will interact with him more in other chapters. He defines *necessity* as "whatever has to be as it is and cannot be otherwise" (*BLW* 149).

In fact, Luther expresses some dissatisfaction with the word *necessity*, precisely because it is usually associated with compulsion, and says he "could wish" for a better word (*BW* 81). Apparently struggling with this, perhaps against the strength of Erasmus's resistance to the word, he distinguishes between two kinds of necessity: the "*necessity of force*, referring to action . . . [and] *necessity of infallibility*, referring to time." Applying this to Judas's betrayal of Jesus, he said, "This act of will in Judas was certainly and infallibly bound to take place" (*BW* 220).

I would suggest that in that very sentence Luther had the better word he sought: *certainty*. On the one hand, I am fairly confident that he really did mean *necessity* in the sense that I have defined it above, given his emphasis on the infallible connection between foreknowledge and foreordination. On the other hand, some of what he says when using that word might as easily have been said about *certainty*.

Luther also spoke of *contingency* (using *contingent* and *contingently*), and an early sentence reveals what determines his use of the word: "God foreknows nothing contingently [but] foresees, purposes, and does all things according to His own immutable, eternal and infallible will" (*BW* 80). His *contingency*, then, is the opposite of *necessity* (*BW* 79, 83–84), and since all things are necessary because they are foreordained by God, there is no real contingency. At the same time, he defines a *contingent* deed rather awkwardly, as "when our will . . . fastens on something presented to us as if by chance, without our having previously thought or planned anything about it" (BW 81). (If, in fact, this were the opposite of his *necessity*, then the latter word might simply mean *deliberately*!)

Edwards does not use the words in exactly the same way as Luther. *Contingency*, he says, originally means what comes to pass by chance or accident. In other words, people use the word when they cannot discern the causes or antecedents of a thing and so it comes to pass without their being able to predict it or incorporate it into their plans. But the word has another meaning, which Edwards adopts: something that comes to pass that *has no connection* with a cause or antecedent and that therefore "has absolutely no previous ground or reason" (FW 155).

Necessity, for Edwards, is the opposite of contingency. Again he distinguishes between the "original" sense of the term and the way it may be used in philosophical reasoning ("terms of art" he calls the latter). Commonly, *necessity* means something that comes to pass in spite of our opposition to it, something we cannot help. But "philosophical necessity" is "nothing else than the full and fixed connection between the things signified by the subject and predicate of a proposition, which affirms something to be true" (FW 153).[3] Here one sees again the rationalistic method of Edwards, in the analysis of propositions and drawing logical inferences from them. He means, of course, that for any sentence (subject and predicate) that states a truth, there must be a *necessary* connection between its subject and predicate; there must be some antecedent in the subject that makes the predicate necessary.

Then, for Edwards, any event—including human volition—that has an antecedent which is the ground or reason for its being what it is, is a *necessary* event. Once again, we see his reliance on the law of cause and effect—even if *cause* is more broadly defined than usual (as already noted), allowing him to distinguish natural necessity from moral necessity. But both kinds are infallibly linked to their causes.

What all this amounts to is that in Edwards's argument *necessity* is little if anything more than *certainty*, as he acknowledges: "Metaphysical or philosophical necessity is nothing different from certainty. I speak not now of the certainty of knowledge, but the certainty that is in things themselves, which is the foundation of the certainty of the knowledge of them; or that wherein lies the ground of the infallibility of the proposition which affirms them" (FW 151–52). Again, he observes that

---

3. The entire discussion (FW 150–55) must be carefully read; Edwards's verbiage sometimes gets in the way.

the only way that anything that is to come to pass hereafter, is or can be necessary is by a connection with something that is necessary in its own nature, or something that already is, or has been; so that the one being supposed, the other *certainly* follows. . . . This is the necessity which especially belongs to controversies about the acts of the will." (*FW* 153–54, italics mine)

Indeed, in a letter that followed publication of *Freedom of the Will*, Edwards observed, "I have largely declared, that the connection between antecedent things and consequent ones . . . which is called moral necessity, is called by the name 'necessity' improperly. . . . Such a necessity as attends the acts of men's will, is more properly called 'certainty'" (*FW* 456).

Two things need to be said about this equation of necessity and certainty. First, the usage is confusing and it would be better if the two words were distinguished. Second, it may very well mean that Edwards is not arguing what his interpreters usually think he is arguing. If indeed, as seems likely, Edwards really means nothing more than that the future is *certain* to be what God knows it to be, then he is in fact not arguing against classic Arminianism on that score. I readily acknowledge that God's absolute foreknowledge of the future, including the volitions of human beings, means to us that everything in the future is certain to be what it will be.

An example of Edwards's reasoning along these lines may help clarify what I am saying. At one point in his discussion, to illustrate his claim that God's knowledge of the future means that the future is necessary, he offers a supposition:

Let us suppose future existences some way or other to have influence back, to produce effects beforehand, and cause exact and perfect images of themselves in a glass [mirror], a thousand years before they exist, . . . that these images are real effects of these future existences, perfectly dependent on, and connected with their cause; . . . this proves . . . that the existence of the things which are their causes, is also equally sure, firm and necessary. (*FW* 266)

And then he observes that, in the same way, God's knowledge of the future is the effect of that future and likewise proves the *necessity* of that future. Once one substitutes the words *certain/certainty* for *necessary/necessity*, any of us can thoroughly agree. *And it is clear that his discussion neither claims nor proves anything more than that.*

His definition of *contingency* likewise leaves something to be desired, being opposed to necessity or to "any fixed and certain connection with some previous ground or reason of its existence" (*FW* 164–65). This means that, for Edwards, contingent events are events without a cause (*FW* 179, 183–84), and since he is certain that all events are caused then contingent events cannot exist (*FW* 214, 216). As already indicated above, Edwards argues that God's certain foreknowledge itself eliminates the possibility of contingency, since (1) nothing can be known without evidence, and a contingency (since it may not be) cannot have evidence; and (2) a contingency is by definition uncertain and God cannot certainly foreknow anything uncertain (*FW* 258–69).

In the end, both Luther and Edwards fail to distinguish clearly between necessity and certainty, and both use *contingency* as though it must be something uncertain. These failures leave the discussion of human volition and foreknowledge not fully explored and allow those theologians to reach a conclusion that comes too quickly.

Foreknowledge and the Future

The question, then, is simply this: Does the fact that God foreknows the future close the door to the future? Does it mean that human beings are unable to choose in any way other than the way God knows they will choose? I am not here dealing with disability from the perspective of human depravity, or with necessity from the perspective of God's foreordination; those discussions are for other chapters. Here the issue is simpler: Does the certainty of a future event, known by God, cancel out the possibility that it could be otherwise?

The answer to this question, regardless how it is asked, requires significant explanation but is relatively simple: no. That something *will* be a certain way does not mean that it *has* to be. To understand this, illustrations are needed. Here's one. Let's say that today, Monday, I am trying to decide which day later this week I will go to the library to return a book I've finished and get another one. My schedule is pretty open; I can go either Thursday or Friday and either choice seems as appealing as the other. That, then, is a contingency. Now let's say, looking into the future, that I decide I will go on Thursday, and in fact I do so. Assuming that to be true, it is just as true and certain on Monday (as it will be on Friday) that I will go on Thursday. Furthermore, God knows that I will go on Thursday. Does this mean that Thursday was the only choice I could have made *because* God knew I would go that day?

Of course not, and I venture to say that almost no one thinks foreknowledge means that. For one thing, knowledge of a fact is not the cause of the fact. Even the knowledge of a future fact is grounded in the fact, not vice versa. God knows I am going on Thursday *only if* in fact I am going on Thursday. If I am going Friday, instead, he knows it that way! When we "assume a future" (and in all such discussions that is what we do), we place ourselves on the other side of that future and, as it were, look back on it as a settled and certain thing. God, of course, can do that from this side of it without his knowledge being in any way causal or what makes it certain. It is not certain because he knows it; he knows it because it is certain. He sees it, in advance, intuitively, but *the future would be certain even if God did not know it* (!)—although such a thing is metaphysically impossible and in that case the world would not exist.

For God to be aware of the future is, in this respect, the same as it is for us to be aware of the past. It is a certain fact that the Confederacy lost the Civil War, but our knowledge of that is not what made it so. Our knowledge of it flows from the certainty of the fact itself. In a way he probably did not intend, Edwards showed us how to view this relationship between (future) facts and knowledge when he supposed that a future event could produce an effect beforehand, one that was viewable in a mirror. In such a case, he said, the future event is the cause and the mirror image viewable beforehand is the effect. In the same way, he says, God's knowledge of the future is the effect of the future (*FW 266*). I don't feel entirely comfortable with the language of cause and effect here, but the relationship he sees is correct: God's knowledge of the future, like our knowledge of the past, is dependent on or grounded in the things known, not vice versa.

Someone will say, then, that just as we cannot now change the past, so the future, already known to God, cannot be changed. I can agree or disagree with that, and here is where that seemingly innocent little word *cannot* comes into play and causes confusion. Yes, *if* one assumes a given future event as certain, then it certainly *will not* be changed and in that sense "cannot" be changed. But one must also be aware that he has already assumed the factuality of the future. Unlike the past, the future is not yet fact. It does not yet exist. It is not yet fixed. That God foresees it does *not* mean that it is already done. In the future are many *contingencies*, things that can be decided in one way or another, and God knows which way they will be decided. But they *will* be decided; they have not yet been decided. And when decision time comes, all possible decisions are just that: possible.

God knows both necessities and contingencies, including the events that will *not* be chosen. He knows what decisions are yet to be made and what those decisions will be. He knows everything that will follow if I decide to go to the library on Thursday, and he knows everything that will follow if I decide to go to the library on Friday. To use the illustration that Erasmus and Luther argued about, he knew that Judas would betray Jesus. But in no way does that simple fact of knowledge settle that Judas *had* to betray him—and the fact that Luther brings foreordination into the discussion may show that he realized this. I do not know whether Judas could have chosen differently, although I assume he could have. But whether he could have or not is not settled by God's foreknowledge of the event. That much is clear.

There is an interesting and significant illustration of God's foreknowledge of contingencies in 1 Samuel 23:1–13. The circumstances are these. David, doing his best to stay beyond Saul's hostile reach, continues to skirmish with the Philistines, who have attacked the village of Keilah. Obtaining the Lord's direction, he and his fighting men go to help and succeed in delivering Keilah from the invaders. Saul finds out where David is and makes preparation to go and capture him there. David learns of this and, seeking God's direction once again, consults Abiathar the priest, who—apparently by means of Urim and Thummim—answers David's questions. The first question is, "Will Saul come down?" The answer: he will. The second question is based on that: "Will the men of Keilah deliver me into Saul's hands?" The answer: they will.

Now, in fact, neither of these two things, *which God foreknew*, came to pass! David and his men left the vicinity. Saul learned that they had gone and did not go to Keilah. And the inhabitants of that village did not betray David to Saul. All these were contingencies, conditional events, and God knew them as contingencies. God knew they would occur only *if* David remained in Keilah, and he answered accordingly. Did God also know that David, once informed, would leave? Of course he did. But that he knew which of two possible sets of events would transpire does not change the fact that there were two possible sets of events and he knew what would transpire regardless which was chosen. It was not *necessary* that David go or stay. The choice was a *contingency* and not settled until it was decided. It was *certain* that those of Keilah would deliver David to Saul if he stayed, and it was *certain* that Saul would not capture him there if he left, and it was *certain* that he would leave. Thus Edwards is right to say that God cannot know uncertainties, but he is wrong to say that contingencies are uncertainties.

There are many such conditional events—contingencies—described in Scripture, even if the state of God's foreknowledge usually remains undescribed behind the scenes and is not often brought to light. I have written, elsewhere, that this event at Keilah is "a better lesson about foreknowledge than any philosophical-theological treatment of the subject that has appeared."[4]

I am the first to acknowledge that some people, including some who agree with me about human volition, find it difficult to grapple with the fact that God knows our choices—as the certainties they are—and yet we can choose differently. I find that reasoning like that which I have given in the preceding paragraphs often does not help them see this. In one sense, one simply has to "see" that the certainty of the future does not make it a necessary future. God knows the choices we will make, but we do not have to make them. Not *all* decisions are that way, of course, but there are decisions to be made when we are not merely free to make the ones we make but able to make different ones. Foreknowledge does not close the door to an open future.

4. Picirilli, "Toward a Non-Deterministic Theology of Divine Providence," 54.

8

Free Will, Human Depravity, and the Grace of God

THAT HUMAN BEINGS, ON this side of the fall, are depraved is a given in Christian theology. Even the church's hymnody does not spare us from this, from both the Arminian and the Calvinistic branches of Reformed theology. Charles Wesley's "Love Divine, All Loves Excelling" pleads with God to "take away our bent to sinning." Robert Robinson's "Come Thou Fount" asks God to "Bind my wand'ring heart to thee" and proceeds to confess, "Prone to wonder, Lord, I feel it, Prone to leave the God I love."

The question is whether this universal and binding human inclination to sin disproves freedom of the will. Luther and Calvin were certain that it does. They spoke of it over and over in their argument against free will, at least as they thought free will was conceived by Arminians. Edwards was no doubt equally certain, but he did not make that a basis for his argument, given that in his work on the subject he chose to take a rationalistic rather than a theological approach.

I am satisfied that depravity is real and total. I am equally satisfied that it does not finally negate the freedom of the will. My purpose in this chapter is to explain this.

Luther and the Bondage of the Will

Erasmus had said, according to Luther, that "the power of 'free-will' is . . . wholly ineffective apart from the grace of God." Luther responds that this is equivalent to saying that the will is not free. Take away that grace and the individual is capable only of evil; thus so-called free will without grace is not

89

free at all but is "the permanent prisoner and bondslave of evil, since it cannot turn itself to good" (*BW* 104). He insists that "you would not call a slave, who acts at the beck of his lord, *free*" (*BW* 137), thus implying that the human will is under the lordship of sin and Satan. Indeed, Luther is alone in emphasizing the role of Satan in all this: "Under his rule the human will is no longer free nor in its own power, but is the slave of sin and of Satan . . . —though, even if Satan did not rule it, sin itself, whose slave man is, would weigh it down enough to make it unable to will good" (*BW* 263). For that matter, it is because of Satan that a person "believes himself to be free, happy, possessed of liberty and ability, whole and alive" (*BW* 162). Such is the miserable estate of the entire human race, and it is all-pervasive. Luther insists that Genesis 8:21 and 6:5 say that human beings are altogether evil "and that nothing but evil is thought of or imagined by man throughout his life" (*BW* 243).

One of the marks of this corruption of humankind, and so one of the reasons for our total inability, is that the natural person is not capable of understanding anything that is of a spiritual nature, as Paul indicates in 1 Corinthians 2:9. Salvation is "incomprehensible to human capacity" (*BW* 139). A "free" will would mean it had power to move itself to act, but that is absurd since it would have "to move itself in the direction of things eternal and incomprehensible to itself" (*BW* 141).

Erasmus and many others would argue that God's commands imply the ability to obey them. Not so, says Luther: God's law merely demonstrates our duty and our inability to do that duty (*BW* 165). For this he cites Romans 3:20, "By the law is knowledge of sin" (*BW* 158). Biblical statements of law are given to make us know our inability.

What this means for Luther, as for Calvin, is that fallen humanity is "free" only to choose evil. Unlike Calvin, Luther preferred not to characterize even this as "free." Both agree that without the Spirit of God a person does evil as a matter of what he wills to do "spontaneously and voluntarily" (*BW* 102). Still, Luther says this is bondage, not freedom: "The will cannot change itself, nor give itself another bent" (*BW* 103), and so the will is not free. "If God is not in us, Satan is, and then it is present with us to will only evil" (*BW* 147).

In light of this, then, what will it take to release people from the bondage of sin and turn them toward God? The answer, for Luther, is God's *grace*. This is, of course, obvious: if people are in a bondage that they cannot break, then if the bondage is to be broken someone from outside must act. Those who are under the corruption of sin are helpless and if they are to be turned God must turn them. That is grace, and "man without grace can will nothing but evil" (*BW* 317). The need for grace, then, must be set in some sort of opposition to free will and Luther believes that to stand for grace he must fight against free will (*BW* 136). "Grace is needed, and the help of grace is given, because 'free-will' of itself can do nothing" (*BW* 270).

Indeed, Luther makes a direct comparison between humanity under grace and humanity under sin. Just as sinful humanity is under the lordship of Satan and consequently is in bondage, not free, so regenerate humanity is under the lordship of God and is in bondage and not free. The regenerate will is not free "to turn elsewhere, or to desire anything else, as long as the Spirit and grace of God remain in a man" (*BW* 103).

Luther's interaction with Erasmus on the need for grace is interesting and tends to raise at least one question. To summarize, Erasmus acknowledges that a person has to have the *help* of grace in order to turn to God. Luther responds by saying that all Erasmus's arguments, however, would support the ability of humans to move toward God without any help at all. For Luther, that is what a "free" will must mean and Erasmus must mean that free will can "by its own power, without grace" apply itself to good and turn itself from evil (*BW* 142). He appears to be saying that if Erasmus *really* believed a person needs the help of grace he could agree with him.

The question, then, is whether Luther would have accepted the idea that depraved human beings could turn to God with the *help* or *assistance* of divine grace, without insisting that regeneration must be logically prior to conversion. Probably not, but he does not make this clear, only suggesting that one of the arguments he does not take time to develop is that the source of grace is the predestinating purpose of God (*BW* 297–98). Calvin himself, however, leaves no doubts that regeneration, as a full work of grace, is needed.

Calvin's View of Human Bondage

Like Luther, Calvin is clear that human nature is so corrupt as a result of the fall that people are not free to turn to God and therefore do not have free will. He affirms that human beings are born with "a perversity derived from inherited corruption" (*BLW* 39), which means that human choices are "held captive" and enslaved by sin as a result of Adam's fall. Adam, by the way, had free will and misused it, losing it for himself and all humankind (*BLW* 46–47). Indeed, since the will is in bondage and cannot therefore be free, even the *saints* (citing Romans 7:23) are "bound as prisoners" until the regenerating work of the Holy Spirit sets them free (*BLW* 68). Calvin's own summary is pointed:

> We allow that man has choice and that it is self-determined, so that if he does anything evil, it should be imputed to . . . his own voluntary choosing. We do away with coercion . . . , because this contradicts the nature of will. . . . We deny that choice is free, because . . . it is of necessity driven to what is evil. . . . We locate the necessity to sin precisely in corruption of the will. (*BLW* 69–70)

Calvin insists that by nature people can only sin (*BLW* 140–41) and that "sin, which it is not in our power to avoid, is nonetheless voluntary" (*BLW* 150). The will, bound by its own corruption, can choose only evil; yet it does so "of its own accord . . . , without being driven by any external impulse" (*BLW* 69).

Unlike Luther, Calvin gives significant attention to the contrast between fallen humanity and our original parents before the fall. In essence, the will before the fall was truly free, and that freedom was lost for the race by the sin of Adam and Eve, a sin in which we all participated in some sense (he does not discuss in what sense). He defines human nature in two ways: first as it was originally when created by God, entirely pure and perfect; then as it is now, corrupted through the fall—for which humankind, not God, is to be blamed (*BLW* 40). When Pighius claimed that some of the fathers had defended free will, Calvin shows that they—Origen, Tertullian, and Irenaeus, specifically (unlike Marcion, who taught that humanity was originally evil)—were defending free will before the fall (*BLW* 70–71).

Calvin observes that the will, being thus corrupted, only "bears fruit which is defiled and unclean," This is not the Creator's fault, he says, but the fault of "original sin"—insisting that all Scripture teaches that God "rightly punished the whole race" for this first sin (*BLW* 186–87).

The question naturally arises, then, as to just how unfallen human beings could fall. Neither Luther nor Calvin focus on this matter, but Edwards does give it some attention, saying that God, in making humankind, so ordered "his circumstances, that from these circumstances, together with his withholding further assistance and divine influence, his sin would infallibly follow" (*FW* 413). Perhaps Luther and Calvin would agree, but that is not certain. It is certain that they would affirm that the fall was incorporated into the plan of God, who works all things, good and evil, toward his designed ends.

Like Luther, Calvin is certain that humanity can be delivered from the corruption of its nature only by the grace of God. This begins with the hearing of the gospel: we preach, but "where someone hears so as to obey, it is a gift of God" (*BLW* 34). Furthermore, the grace involved is not mere *assistance* but regeneration itself; he criticizes Jerome for not having taught that the liberty lost in the fall is recovered only through the grace of regeneration (*BLW* 77–78). Calvin cites the Council of Orange to label as a heretic anyone who denies this and so teaches that faith, whether in its initiation or continuation, is anything other than a gracious gift of God (*BLW* 82).

Indeed, Calvin takes this one step farther. This grace of God does not merely work in such a way as to make it possible for the person to choose or reject it, but God "moves the will also effectively to obedience, he . . . advances the endeavor until the actual completion of the work is attained" (*BLW* 114).

In other words, for Calvin, grace is more than an aid in our helplessness, leaving some part dependent on us. Instead, it is an entire work by which our wills are made new and "effectively formed" so that we "necessarily" respond and obey (*BLW* 174).

Furthermore, this grace of regeneration is better than the grace Adam had before the fall, which meant that he could choose to remain in God's will or abandon it. We have grace that causes us to will to remain (*BLW* 133; cf. 177–78). The original freedom of Adam and Eve was "to be able not to sin"; ours is better: "not to be able to sin" (*BLW* 240). This grace is absolutely and wholly effective. And it is administered sovereignly. Though a person "acts," he "acts in such a way that the effectiveness of the action is . . . entirely in the control of the Spirit of God" (*BLW* 172).

Indeed, this grace "is bestowed by the good pleasure of God" and so only on those whom he has chosen (*BLW* 240). Furthermore, it includes necessary perseverance. The work of grace "actually makes people believers, which not only provides the means for persevering, but equips them with enough steadfastness for them to do nothing but persevere" (*BLW* 243–44).

Responding to the Argument from Depravity and Grace

Is the human race totally depraved? And does this fact mean that free will has been lost? And in that case does this mean that to be saved by God's grace rules out the ability of humans to choose or reject that grace? These three questions hang together closely.

Depravity

There is no need to disagree with Luther and Calvin about the fact that the whole human race, as a result of the fall, inherits a nature so corrupted and in bondage to sin that turning to God (conversion) is not possible apart from an initiating work of God's grace.

This depravity is *universal*, in that no human being is excepted—other than the God-man himself, Jesus Christ. It is beyond my purpose, here, to venture into extended discussion of the *basis* on which the guilt and condemnation for the sin of Adam and Eve is justly imputed by God to the whole race. Some Reformed theologians ground this in "natural headship": the fact that we were all physically "in the loins of" Adam when he sinned, and so—as Levi paid tithes in the loins of Abraham (Hebrews 7:9–10)—we all sinned in Adam. Others ground this in "federal headship," contending that God covenanted with Adam to be the head of the human race and so to represent us all in obedience or disobedience, thus making us all guilty when he sinned.

I do not find either approach entirely satisfactory, but I wholeheartedly accept the truth that in some sense best understood by God we all participated in Adam's sin and as a result we came to experience all the penalties of that sin, including condemnation, death, and depravity. It seems clear that Romans 5:12–19 teaches this, and that verse 12, in saying "all have sinned" (AV), means we "all sinned" (a Greek aorist) when Adam sinned. In the final analysis, if it were unjust to count us all as guilty of that sin, it would be equally unjust to punish us all with the death and depravity that are consequent to it. But that is not unjust, and God knows exactly why.

Paul rightly says, then, "There is none who does good, no not one" (Romans 3:12), where he recites a lengthy litany of similar pronouncements from the Psalms and Isaiah. They include Psalm 14, which portrays God as looking down from heaven to see if there are any among humans who have the understanding needed to seek God; and there are *none*. "They have *all* turned aside" (v. 3), reminding us of Isaiah 53:6: "We have turned every one to his own way." These passages—and there are many more—make clear to us that the human race is by nature wicked to the core. As Jeremiah 17:9 affirms, "The heart is deceitful above all things, and desperately wicked." For these last two words some suggest "incurably sick," an appropriate rendering.

This depravity is likewise *total*. Most interpreters of Scripture and the human condition will acknowledge that this does not mean that every individual is as evil as he or she is capable of becoming. It does mean, however, that every part of human nature is evilly affected by the fall, whether the mind, the desires, or the will. Fallen human beings are not able to understand spiritual things, are controlled by wicked passions, and make their choices under inclinations and influences that are contrary to the ways of God. Left to themselves, no persons will ever turn to God.

This does not mean that there is nothing noble about human beings after Eden. Humanity is a mixed bag, a walking set of tensions between great achievements and wicked ambitions. Various human beings have accomplished wonderful and admirable things in the arts, in deeds of self-sacrifice, in charitable acts and institutions, in the conquest of diseases, and in many other areas. At the same time, human beings have shown a propensity for incredible depths of wickedness, in human trafficking, in atrocities associated with war, in the ovens of Auschwitz, in supreme selfishness, and in many other areas. The contradiction involved in this can only be explained by viewing human beings both as created in the image of God and as fallen into sinful corruption and rebellion against their Maker.

So human beings continue to reflect the image of God, regardless how fallen, and are capable of great good as viewed from our flawed perspective. At the same time, they are estranged from their Creator. They do not know him and do not want to know him. They have declared their independence from him and love their sins. In their separation from God they cannot understand and do not find appealing the vision that God has for them. They are blind and deaf and dead, and (in full agreement with Luther and Calvin) in that condition they cannot by any act of their wills, by any volition or decision, turn themselves toward God.

As Jesus expressed this, "No one can come to Me unless the Father who sent Me draws him" (John 6:44). Total depravity, faced with a *mere* "gospel" offer of deliverance by the redemptive work of Jesus, is helpless and entirely unable to respond.

Prevenient Grace

Luther, Calvin, and Edwards, faced with what I have just described, decided that the only answer to the dilemma is to be found in the immediate and intervening regeneration of the individual by grace. There is a certain logic to this: if humankind is helpless to will in favor of God—if they are dead and deaf, blind and in bondage—then God must *first* change them before he can expect them to make any decision or choice in God's favor. This, for Calvin at least, is *prevenient* grace.

The word *prevenient* means "going before, preceding, anticipating, antecedent to," reflecting an older meaning, no longer in use, of the verb *prevent* (as in 1 Thessalonians 4:15, AV). Pighius had referred to the role of "prevenient grace" in preparing the sinner to turn to God, but Calvin insists that prevenient grace includes actually making the will good (*BLW* 194–95)—the grace of regeneration, in other words. For Calvin, God must take the initiative of grace in order to save a person who is spiritually dead, and that first step is to make the person over from the inside out by regeneration.

I would suggest that this is not a good biblical-theological step to take. Once taken, it guarantees what we may call a "limited and unconditional" election of who will be saved. If regeneration is the first step, then human beings are not only *unable* to make a choice, they *have* no choice at all. God will regenerate those whom he chooses to save, and the others will be given no opportunity for grace.

More important, Calvin's step is an unnecessary one. Prevenient grace—God's initiating grace that precedes all human endeavor—need not be regeneration. To be sure, humanity is so depraved and in such circumstances that, left to ourselves, we will never turn toward God, and this means that God must take the first step and extend grace to us. In one sense, of course, God has already done that in sending his Son to die for our sins and arise from the dead for our justification (Romans 4:25). But God's act in history, by itself, would not bring any sinner to himself. More is required, and this is where prevenient grace comes into play in the theology of salvation. It has, in the main, two parts: the Word and the Spirit.

One: The Word is the proclamation of the gospel. One of Calvinism's mistakes, I believe, lies in not giving the Word of God the place it deserves in the salvation of the lost. For Calvinists, regeneration not only does not require the Word, but indeed the Word cannot be heard until after regeneration. And since all else in salvation infallibly flows from regeneration, then the Word has no *essential* place in salvation. In theory, at least, some elect could go to heaven without ever hearing the Word.

The New Testament, in contrast, places the Word at the very heart of the application of salvation to an individual. Romans 10:10–17 provides the theological basis for this. Paul explains that one must believe—exercise faith—in one's heart in order to be saved and then begins a line of rhetorical questions devoted to making his point: How can one believe if he has not heard? And how can one hear unless another preaches the Word of the gospel? And how can anyone preach without being sent? Conclusion: "Faith comes by hearing, and hearing by the word of God" (v. 17). As 1 Peter 1:23 indicates, the new birth itself is "through the word of God."

The New Testament, then, reflects this fundamental relationship a number of times, either in reporting history or in explicating it. Acts 4:4 reports that "many of those who heard the word believed." Ephesians 1:13 expounds this very order: you *heard* the word of truth of the gospel, you *trusted* in Christ, and you *received* the Holy Spirit as a seal and earnest. John 5:24 represents the same order: "He who hears My word and believes in Him who sent Me has everlasting life." Acts 10:44, in this light, has powerful implications: "While Peter was still speaking these words, the Holy Spirit fell upon all those who heard the word."

We must not overlook the power of the Word of God in its own right. As Psalm 119:130 exclaims, "The entrance of Your words gives light." Hebrews 4:12 reports that "the word of God is living and powerful," sharper than a double-edged sword and cutting deeply into one's thoughts and heart. Paul observes that Jesus gave himself for the church with the purpose to sanctify and "cleanse it with the washing of water by the word" (Ephesians 5:26). Jesus, citing Deuteronomy 8:3, urges that "man shall not live by bread alone, but by every word that proceeds from the mouth of God" (Matthew 4:4). In his great high-priestly prayer Jesus prayed to the Father to sanctify his disciples by the truth, adding, "Your word is truth" (John 17:17). In Colossians 1:5–6 Paul recites how "the word of the truth of the gospel" had come to his readers and "is bringing forth fruit . . . since the day you heard and knew the grace of God in truth."

Biblical evidence for this line of thought could go on at great length, but I will resist the temptation—except to say that a careful reading of the book of Acts alone should convince any discerning reader of the primary and essential place of hearing the Word proclaimed in God's plan to bring salvation to people. And it should be just as clear that there is no "hidden" assumption underlying all these evangelistic accounts, to the effect that they were bringing the Word to people already regenerated.

Two: The convicting work of the Holy Spirit is complementary and essential to the effectiveness of the Word of God in bringing sinners to God. Paul observes that the Word of God is "the sword of the Spirit." It is the Spirit who wields this "sword" and brings the conviction that enables faith. The *mere* hearing of the gospel will not by itself constitute the gracious work of God necessary to bring depraved hearers to faith. The Holy Spirit must be at work to convict, enlighten, and persuade.

Jesus promised that the work of the Spirit would be to "convict the world of sin, and of righteousness, and of judgment" (John 16:8). The word *convict* (Greek *elegchō*) suggests the idea of rebuke or reproach, to make a statement grounded in proof. Our English word *convict* has the same root as *convince*, and this fits the meaning well. The work of the Holy Spirit includes using the Word of God to convince people of their guilt, and of the judgment, and of the nature and need of righteousness. At least that much is indicated by Jesus' words. It seems likely that 1 John 5:6 refers to this same ministry: "It is the Spirit who bears witness, because the Spirit is truth."

Consequently, Paul was correct, when describing to Roman believers his preaching ministry, to include as one of its characteristics that it was "by the power of the Spirit of God" (Romans 15:19). Similarly, in 1 Thessalonians 1:4, looking back on his time in Thessalonica, he says that his gospel "did not come to you in word only, but also in power, and in the Holy Spirit." Again, he reminds the Corinthians that his "speech and preaching," while he was among them, was "not with persuasive words of human wisdom, but in demonstration of the Spirit and of power, that your faith should not be in the wisdom of men but in the power of God" (1 Corinthians 2:4–5).

In summary, there is a preregenerating, enabling grace that is brought to bear on the depraved, dead, blind, and bound sinner, and it is operative by the Word of God and the work of the Spirit of God. This is apparently what Acts 16:14 is referring to when it reports of Lydia, the seller of purple from Thyatira, that "the Lord opened her heart." It would be *possible* that this refers to regeneration, but it is more likely that it refers to a work of grace that made it possible for her to understand and believe—when in her depravity without that work of grace she would never have believed. In this the sweet winds of grace were blowing as she heard Paul's teaching, and this is what I have referred to a number of times in my discussion of the biblical basis for free will in chapter 3.

It probably should not surprise us that something short of regeneration can enable faith. As depraved as one is, he is still a person, a human being in the image of God. Sinners are spiritually blind, but the Word and the Spirit can bring them to see the truth of the gospel. They are spiritually dead, which does not mean they have ceased to exist as persons, but, instead, that they are separated from and do not know God—but still have that capacity. The Holy Spirit can wield the Word so as to "draw" sinners in spite of their deadness—and in all likelihood the Father's drawing (John 6:44) is done by the work of the Spirit. The sinner is spiritually deaf, but the Holy Spirit, using the Word of God, can cause the deaf to hear. In other words, the Spirit and the Word can persuade a person of the truths needed for that person to be able to receive the gift of salvation offered in the gospel. That is not a hard thing for the Lord. Nothing is too hard for the Lord!

"Where the Spirit of the Lord is, there is liberty," says Paul in 2 Corinthians 3:17. I don't think it stretches the implications of this too much to suggest that the liberty of the will is included, which leads to the final point of this chapter. It is a corrupted will, a will in bondage to sin, but it is a will yet. And the grace of God enables a decision that would otherwise be impossible.

Has Fallen Humanity Lost Free Will?

I have already anticipated the answer to this, but some additional observations are required in order to make the answer clear and convincing.

Start with what I've indicated in a previous chapter. Free will is nothing more than the power of choice, understood as a real power to choose either of two (or more) alternatives. A "will" is, by definition, such a power of choice and so "free." Free will is not some part of a person, like his body or his mind. It is a way a *person* functions, a capacity or power possessed by a person. The fall did not destroy that capacity or ability. The *person* is bound by sin and his depraved nature, and thus his ability to will is seriously affected. But his will has not been destroyed.

What the fall did was to change the circumstances of all people's existence, not just externally but internally. They became spiritually dead, being cut off from the knowledge and presence of God. They became depraved, strongly inclined to wickedness. Every *person* became bound by his or her own passions for evil, blinded to truth and to the appeal of a relationship with God, headstrong in the pursuit of their own selfish indulgences. In those circumstances, as Luther and Calvin said, they could choose only against God. No person, left alone, would ever choose for God in those circumstances, depraved and deceived.

Depraved human beings can be compared to a woman in jail. She has not lost the ability to walk about freely outside, but her circumstances limit that freedom and prevent her from doing so. Calvin said that a freedom that can't be exercised isn't freedom; the statement is understandable and "practically" true, but it isn't "theoretically" true.

In the same way, fallen humanity has not lost the capacity or ability to choose. We may not see things clearly enough to choose intelligently.

We may be so bound by our own passions that our choices are always evil. But if some Power outside us can show us the truth of our condition and of the means and offer of deliverance, we will be enabled to make a choice we could not otherwise make. This is prevenient grace, the work of the Holy Spirit inhabiting and empowering the proclaimed Word. By it the otherwise disabled sinner is enabled to accept or reject the gospel offer of salvation by Jesus Christ.

I have said, more than once, that persons *left to themselves* are not able in their circumstances to turn toward God. What we are grateful for is that God *has not left us to ourselves*. He has taken the double initiative of providing grace—grace that precedes anything we do. He has bought our redemption by the work of Jesus, and he has given his Word and Spirit to make the message plain and convincing.

A Final Question: Does God Force the Will?

As I have noted above, both Luther and Calvin insist that, in this work of regenerating grace, God does not force the human will. This strikes me as such an inconsistency that I cannot help wondering why it seems important to them to say this in spite of that. I do not wish to pursue this at great length, but a few observations seem warranted.

To put it simply: if, in fact, the person being regenerated is, *up to the instant when regeneration takes place*, unwilling to seek God, then regeneration comes against the person's will. In that case, then, the will is being forced or coerced. Saying that this is not the case is entirely unconvincing. One can utter a set of words, to be sure, but if everything else one says contradicts what those words affirm, then the observer realizes that the affirmation is suspiciously hollow. I think this is what applies to the utterances of Luther and Calvin that deny force or coercion.

According to both Luther and Calvin, then, and Edwards for that matter, depravity is of such a nature that every person in the world wills only sin and willingly resists the conquest of his heart by God. Furthermore, they affirm that there can be no change in this resistance *until regeneration takes place*. The person must be changed from within before he or she can submit to God, and only in regeneration does this change take place. Until regeneration, then, there is nothing in any of us that is contrary to the inclinations of our depraved nature. Our wills are against submission to God, and so God must change us against our wills.

The view of the will and of prevenient grace that I have set forth in this chapter does not face this same problem. In this view, the *capacity* for choice has not been lost, but depravity has so affected all people's nature and circumstances that they do not understand or desire any way other than the sinful way they love. Against the person's willing resistance to God, then, comes the Word of the gospel of salvation, under the conviction of the Holy Spirit, and opens blind eyes to another choice, an appealing choice that he or she did not realize was open. And the sweet, inviting influence of grace, by that persuasive call to the dead sinner, makes it possible to choose for God or to reject the opportunity for reconciliation to him. Truly, then, the sinner is brought to God—drawn but not dragged—without the coercion of the will.

9

Free Will and the Sovereignty
and Providence of God

IN THE CHAPTER ON Calvin I noted that one of his three main reasons for rejecting free will, as he thought Pighius and the Roman Catholics understood it, was the all-encompassing government of God. All three of our principals, Luther, Calvin, and Edwards, would insist on this, touting the closely interwoven doctrines of the sovereignty of God, the universal efficacy of his eternal decrees, and so his providential control of every event—including every human volition—in the history of the world.

It would be foolish to shrink from the fact that God is sovereign and that his providential government of the cosmos includes all of the choices human beings make. Satan himself is wholly subject to God's government and can do nothing other than what God's will for him encompasses—as the drama involving Job confirms. If that is true for Satan, it is at least as true for us.

Does that negate freedom of the will? Our three theologians were confident that it does.

Luther and the Sovereignty of God

One of the things Luther does is use Proverbs 16:1 and 21:1—"the king's heart is in the hand of the Lord . . . he turns it wherever he wishes"—to argue for the sovereignty of God over humankind. On the second of these Erasmus had said, "He who inclines does not forthwith compel." Luther responds that he is speaking not of compulsion but of the "necessity of immutability," which "is meant by the 'inclining' of God, which is . . . the most active operation of God, which man cannot avoid or alter." In this circumstance the person has "the will which God gave him, and which God now makes to act by His own movement" (BW 258–59).

Erasmus had argued for God's *permission*, to which Luther responds by urging that whether one speaks of permitting or inclining, "the king's will cannot escape the action of the omnipotent God by which all men's wills, good and bad, are moved to will and to act" (BW 259). He cites "Balaam's inability to say what he wished" as a clear example in Scripture (BW 259).

Along similar lines, Luther says that Paul, in Romans 9:11–13, rightly quoted Malachi 1:2–3 to prove the sovereignty of God in grace. Erasmus had maneuvered around this by saying it dealt with matters of standing and privilege, not with saving grace. Luther rejects this approach, perhaps correctly. He acknowledges that people are saved by faith and rejected by unbelief, but then he insists that "Paul teaches that faith and unbelief come to us by no work of our own, but through the love and hatred of God" (BW 228–29).

Luther's keyword for God's role in all events, including salvation, is *omnipotence*. By this he does not mean to say simply that God is all-powerful or able to do anything in keeping with his character. For him, if God is all-powerful that must mean that God actually does all things. He defines God's omnipotence as "the active power by which He mightily works all in all" (BW 217). "Man without the grace of God nonetheless remains under the general omnipotence of the God who effects, and moves, and impels all things" (BW 265).

This is true for the unconverted, even though they are under Satan's mastery. "He works all things in all men, even in the ungodly; for He alone moves, makes to act, and impels by the motion of His omnipotence, all those things which He alone created; they can neither avoid nor alter this movement, but necessarily follow and obey it" (BW 267). This is likewise true for the saints: "When God acts by the Spirit of His grace in those whom He has justified . . . He moves and carries them along in like manner; and they . . . follow and co-operate with Him, or rather, as Paul says, are made to act by Him (Rom. 8:14)" (BW 267).

One cannot overlook the importance, in these assertions, of "God actually does all things," or that all persons "are made to act by Him." Even Judas's betrayal of Jesus, Luther says, "was the work of God, brought into being by His omnipotence, like everything else" (BW 213).

This concept of omnipotence Luther links with foreknowledge (see my chapter 7 and BW 216–18) and concludes, with strong assertions, that once these two are granted it is entirely clear that there is no such thing as free will and that everything we do God "works by His infallible and immutable counsel and power" (*BW* 218).

Calvin and God's All-Encompassing Government

Although the terminology is somewhat different, Calvin's view is essentially the same as Luther's. He observes, for example, that "God is in charge of the world." This means that, for human beings, God "bends their wills this way and that in accordance with his choice," that they do only what God has decreed, regardless what "they may try to do" (*BLW* 38). He immediately adds that things that seem to us to happen by chance really happen by necessity since God's purpose "is sovereign in governing them." Both the ends and the means to these ends, which Calvin calls "secondary causes," serve to fulfill the divine purpose.

The idea of sovereignty involves freedom. For Calvin, God's grace could not be called *free* unless it is bestowed only on those whom he sovereignly chooses (*BLW* 200). In connection with this, Calvin notes that Pighius found it difficult to extol the goodness of God without seeing it as made available to all. For Calvin this is repugnant. God's mercy "shines better" when he demonstrates it in some while at the same time demonstrating "his wrath and judgment" in others (*BLW* 200). If some *reason* for this difference should be sought, Calvin replies that the decision must rest with the potter and not the clay; indeed, God has a reason, but it "is too secret . . . and concealed . . . to be grasped by the measure of our mind" (*BLW* 191).

For Calvin, then, the all-encompassing providence of God extends to every event: "Human affairs are . . . controlled by the fixed purpose of God"; everything created, "either of its own accord or under coercion," obeys God "of necessity, as he has ordained" (*BLW* 39).

Furthermore, Calvin cannot accept that this sovereign governance of God allows a human being to play the part of one who chooses or rejects grace. The work of grace, then, must be effective and not merely enabling (*BLW* 174, 177).

In other words, for Calvin, grace is offered only to be effective (*BLW* 195). Calvin cites Augustine on the matter of who produces salvation, saying it is "God whom no human choice resists when he wants to make it whole" (*BLW* 239). He also agrees with Augustine that saving grace is extended only to those whom he has chosen for that purpose (*BLW* 240).

God's work does more than restore ability, it "actually makes people believers" (*BLW* 243–44).

Edwards and Divine Sovereignty

As I have indicated, Edwards does not rely on the traditional theological arguments, choosing instead to mount a rationalistic defense against free will. Even so, he no doubt would have agreed wholeheartedly with Luther and Calvin in their reliance on the all-encompassing government of God as ruling out the possibility of true freedom of the will.

Regardless, he does indicate his view of the sovereignty of God when he responds to the objection that his view is like the Stoic doctrine of fate or the philosophy of Hobbes. He holds, instead, to the view of

> the world's being in all things subject to the disposal of an intelligent wise agent, that presides, not as the soul of the world, but as the sovereign Lord of the universe, governing all things by proper will, choice and design, in the exercise of the most perfect liberty conceivable, without subject to any constraint, or being properly under the power or influence of anything before, above or without himself. (*FW* 374)

But he does not use this as an argument against freedom of the will.

Sovereignty, Providence, and Free Will

Luther and Calvin, and no doubt Edwards, were confident that God's sovereign government of the world rules out free will if free will is taken to mean the power to choose for or against God. Were they right? Does God's sovereign, all-encompassing providence mean that it is not possible for a person to choose other than what he chooses? I am satisfied that the answer is negative, and my purpose in this chapter is to show why I can say that with confidence.

The Meaning and Implications of God's Sovereignty

Just above I have quoted Edwards's view of God's sovereign government of the world. I trust it will come as no surprise for me to say that there is not a single thing there to disagree with. The key elements of his definition are (1) that God is sovereign lord of the universe; (2) that he governs all things by his own will; (3) that he does so in complete liberty; and (4) that this includes his being without any obligation to anything or anyone other than himself. A biblical view of things requires that we affirm each of these elements.

That God's government is all-inclusive I will discuss below under the heading of providence. I focus, here, on the primary truths involved in understanding God's sovereignty. To be a sovereign or have sovereignty, in general, means to rule above all others, and so to have the final authority. It includes the idea of being completely free to do as one wills without having to condition one's decisions by what others think or do.

The sovereignty of God, then, involves at least three main things. First is the fact that he governs the world in perfect freedom. As Psalm 115:3 expresses this, "Our God is in heaven; He does whatever He pleases." There is no condition attached to this, and no limitation. Nothing restricts God's liberty to do exactly as he chooses. No other being in the universe enjoys such sovereignty.

The second thing is implied in the first: he is under no obligation to any being or idea, other than himself, to act in a certain way. I include "idea" in this because sometimes philosophers discuss, for example, whether things are good because God does them or he does them because they are good. Neither is true: the very meaning of *good* is determined by his own character and he always acts in accord with his character. So there is no concept—no eternal *idea* or *form* or *universal*, in some Platonic sense—outside God that conditions his actions. Just as he acts freely without being under obligation to any concept grounded in some reality other than himself, so he is under no obligation to any of the things he has created, including human beings. He owes us nothing. He is perfectly free, and able, to act as he chooses. To be sure, God is bound to act justly in all relationships, but that obligation is to himself. We do not impose it on him nor is there some preexisting concept of justice that he must respect.

The third thing involved in this is that God has complete control over everything that transpires in the world, including the choices and actions of human beings. His rule encompasses all events. Nothing is outside his dominion. He has not lost control. Everything takes place within the all-embracing compass of his willingness and contributes, in a way he has designed, to the accomplishment of his ultimate purpose, which cannot be thwarted.

Some of these things appear obvious when one thinks about the implications. Regardless what else is to be said, surely no being—not even

Satan, the master enemy himself—can finally thwart the purpose of God. Equally sure, it is not possible for God to lose control over his world.

What does *control* mean, then? It does not mean that God does or causes everything in the universe that occurs. It does mean, for everything that occurs, that (1) God knows about it, from eternity; (2) that he provides for it in such a manner as to regulate it; and (3) that he fits it perfectly into his plan for things. In the case of human beings, whom God created to bear his image, God has granted a limited freedom to be actors, to "originate" events by their own unconstrained decisions. But he knows them all, regulates the exercise of their freedom in ways that do not negate their liberty, and incorporates all their choices and acts into his government of the created order.

What does it mean, then, that God controls all things *according to his predetermined will, his foreknowledge and foreordination*? Working toward an answer, I first pose a question to anyone who believes in the all-encompassing control of God. Do you mean that in eternity (before the foundation of the world) God made and adopted a plan? That in his planning he determined to create Adam and Eve in Eden and set before them life and death? That he knew that if he did this the way he did, they would certainly disobey and plunge the race into spiritual death and depravity? That he determined, therefore, to provide redemption and incorporated all of this into a plan that assuredly will not fail to succeed as he meant it to succeed? Do you mean, furthermore, that he foreknew, even then (among uncountable other things), that the Germans under Hitler would exterminate millions of Jews in "the final solution"? That he also foreknew, even then, that the Roman church would slip its moorings and Luther would rise up to call a people out from that apostasy, and that among those who responded there would be Arminians arguing for a universal provision and Calvinists arguing against it? That he knew, from the very beginning, and lovingly identified as his own, those who would believe in his Son, and grievingly consigned the rest to hell? That, in summary, he saw all the possibilities, knowing the ones that would certainly occur, and said, in effect, "That is what we will have! Let that come about!"?

If that is what one means in insisting that everything in the world goes according to God's plan, or is in accord with his sovereign will, then who can possibly disagree? I certainly do not. Yes, God knew that Adam would sin. He knew that all would sin. He knew that as a result of sin there would be universal death and depravity and miseries untold. He knew that some would be redeemed and that some would not, that some would spend eternity with him in unimaginable blessedness, and that others would spend eternity hopelessly separated from him and from all joy. Knowing all that would transpire, including each individual's life and destiny, he said, "Let that be the case" and set in motion the things that would certainly bring all this to pass.

How, then, does acknowledging this cohere with passages like 2 Peter 3:9, which affirms that God is "not willing that any should perish"? Can God will both that some be saved and others not, and at the same time not will that any should perish? Apparently so. Indeed, anyone who believes the Scriptures, which tell us both that God does not will that any perish and that many will perish, must allow for this difficulty. If some are going to hell, then God's will must include that reality in some sense. All theologians, then, of whatever persuasion about free will, end up making some sort of distinctions in God's will.

In one way of looking at his will, he assigns to eternal punishment those who reject him and thus "wills" that some perish. In another way of looking at his will, he does not desire that any perish. In two different senses, then, his will is expressed in both of these. Various theologians have tried various terms for making this distinction, and I leave that to them, suggesting simply that in some things God's will is unconditional and absolute and in other things his will is conditional. Our understanding of this is helped, to some degree, by the fact that all of us experience, at times, a similar difference within our own wills.

I have said little about foreordination or predestination in this discussion, so I hasten to add now that to speak of this is no more than to say what I have said about God's plan adopted before the foundation of the world. Theologians typically define the elements of that foreordained plan as *decrees*, which means nothing more than the decisions God made as parts of his plan. There is no good reason to object to this or to avoid attempting to define the decisions of God that were incorporated in the eternal plan he had in mind when he created the cosmos and humanity. Even so, there is every good reason to be sure that in such discussion we do not give, to those who hear us, the impression that *the interaction between God and human beings in time* is unreal or of secondary importance. To do that is to do a disservice to the church and world and to distort the biblical record.

The fact is that God acts in time and space, right along with us. Whatever the date was, he created Adam and Eve at specific times and places, not in eternity. He set life and death before them then and there, and he judged them after their sin, not before. He had Samuel anoint Saul as king (knowing he would disobey and forfeit the honor) at a particular juncture in Israel's history. And he took from Saul his Spirit after Saul's disobedience, and not until then. He redeemed Israel from Egypt at the time of a certain Pharaoh and would have taken them into Canaan forty years before he finally did if they had not disobeyed. He fought for them and gave them possession of the land during one period, and during subsequent periods he brought in the Assyrians, first, and then Nebuchadnezzar of Babylon to take them away, and did so as a result of the fact that they had gone after idols.

Did God's eternal plan incorporate all these interactions? Yes. But we must not look at the actual history and think that it is some sort of predetermined rehearsal after the fact, merely playing out in motion what has already been settled. To do that is to miss the whole message of the Bible, which is that God deals with us in time and space. He speaks and we obey or disobey, and he responds accordingly *when we do*. He sets before us life and death *now*, and we choose *now*. Is there a sense in which he "decided" to do all these things in eternity? Yes. But *he did not "do" them then; he does them now*. And he does them now *in response* to what we do. The action between God and humanity is in the world that humanity occupies, for good or ill. God acts and human beings respond. People act and God responds. That is the story of the Bible. And in that story it is not God alone who acts, but the beings he created in his image act, too. God is not the only actor in the universe; so are we. And it is entirely inadequate for someone to *say* that he believes that human beings act, too, and then to say other things that in effect contradict that.

If someone suggests that God is too transcendent to act in space and time, we need only to use two words to disprove them: *creation* and *incarnation*. But for that matter the whole history of the Bible disproves them. Foreordination, yes, but not so as to detract from the interaction of God and humanity in this real world of time and space that he made and situated us in. Affirming God's sovereignty, or that his plan is being accomplished, does not therefore mean we need to give up free will or universal provision.

I will return to this after discussing divine providence.

The Meaning and Implications of God's Providence

I will not attempt, here, to treat thoroughly the doctrine of providence. I have done some of that elsewhere.[1] At this point I will discuss only those aspects of

1. Picirilli, "Toward a Non-Deterministic Theology of Divine Providence," 38–61).

the doctrine that bear on the present discussion of free will, beginning with a definition of providence. Most simply put, the providence of God is his work in providing for the created order. More formally, providence is the activity of God in caring for and governing the universe in accord with his unfailing purpose. This discussion, then, is closely related to the preceding discussion about sovereignty. I will try to avoid much repetition.

One of the more important facets of this doctrine is that God's providence encompasses everything that transpires. This includes all the events that we would categorize as belonging to natural law as well as the free choices made by persons. That all of this is embraced in God's providential control is obvious. It is also scriptural. Romans 8:28 affirms, "We know that all things work together for good to those who love God, to those who are the called according to His purpose." Isaiah 45:9–10 agrees: "I am God, and there is none like me, declaring the end from the beginning, and from ancient times the things that are not yet done, saying, My counsel shall stand, and I will do all my pleasure." He is the governor of all things and directs them all to his appointed ends and apparently to the welfare of those whom he identifies as his. Nothing is too small or too large for this to apply. Everything is included. Everything.

Even so, as already noted, his *control* does not mean that God actively performs or desires or causes everything that is done. His control only requires, as defined above, that he knows and provides for every event to be governed by his plan. If he is not the only actor in the universe—and he is not: there are others whom he has made in his image and given that capacity—he still rules their actions and directs them according to his will.

Louis Berkhof, representing the Calvinist wing of Reformed theology, defines God's providence as including three elements: *preservation*, that God maintains the existence, nature, and powers of all things he created; *concurrence*, that he acts in all the acts of his creatures, so that nothing transpires independently of him; and *government*, that he is at work in everything so as to accomplish his purpose.

The most debatable of these is *concurrence*, which is used in this context to mean more than mere agreement. Here it means acting together with, and the question is whether God acts together with every person in everything a person does. So long as we limit discussion to something physical—like laying a brick or steering an automobile or signing a contract—the matter does not concern us greatly. We have no trouble understanding that every step we take requires the sustaining activity of God, or that every breath is from his hand.

But human beings do more than physical things; they also *sin*. Does God sin with them or *concur* in their sins? The answer is that he does not. He may sustain the elements in a murderer's bullet and the laws of physics that are involved in the bullet's flight and death of the victim. But the murderer does something that God does not do with him: he sins. It is important for us to recognize that to *sin* is to do something very different from a physical act. Sin (like any act with moral qualities) is something only a *person* can do, and it is done only in the inner being: in the mind or heart, in the motive or intent or *will*. In one sense, only choosers sin, only choices are sins (or goods).

It is better to say, then, that God does not concur with the sinner in his sin, else we would make God himself a sinner. One may strive to make *concur* mean something else, but if so it will probably be better to find a different word. For that matter, regardless how sophisticated we may be in our choice and use of words, it will be much better if we insist that God does nothing that makes it necessary for a person to sin, else he becomes the cause or author of evil.

Did God make Adam and Eve in such a way that they were *capable* of sin? Of course. Did he make them by nature and in circumstances where they *had* to sin? No. Did he make them knowing that if he did, and put them in the circumstances they were in, they would sin? Yes. Did he reckon with that and make sure it was incorporated in his wise and good plan for the created order and the human race? Most certainly. Why did he do that, knowing that sin would result and the human race would be cast into death and depravity? Only he knows the answer to that; we can only speculate. At the same time, we are satisfied that God rules supreme, governing all things—including sin and Satan—for his own good purposes.

I do not think I need to pursue this at greater length, except perhaps to add that this leaves us with the fact that everything in the universe other than God must be traced back, ultimately, to God. This includes the existence of evil (although it is not a "thing" in the usual sense of the word). And this, in turn, apparently means that when God created human beings and gave them freedom to choose to obey or disobey him, that capacity opened the door of the world to evil. Evil—like all moral value—lies specifically within the free, responsible choices of persons. Nowhere else is there evil in a moral sense.

We are compelled to take by faith, then, the fact that God has acted righteously to allow sin in his world. And no amount of theological or philosophical finagling will allow us to avoid that God has done this. Some, like the open theists, have suggested that if God knew the Holocaust was coming, he would have been under obligation to stop it—or else in some way he would be an accessory to the evil. Not so: he most certainly knew, when the Jews were forced like cattle into the railway cars and shuttled off to the ovens, what *was* happening, and he did not stop it then. There is no better word than *permission* to use for his allowance of this, and it violates everything biblical to say (or even to use words that sound like) he "did" this atrocity. Did he "govern" the extermination of the Jews? Yes. Was he still in control? Yes. Why did he allow it? God knows. How does it contribute to his plan? I have no answer and I am not embarrassed by that.

Does God Save Only Those Whom He Pleases?

The answer, unequivocally, is yes. But the answer does not tell us whom he pleases to save! What we have seen, above, about God's sovereignty and providence is that God governs all events in the world in accord with his plan. He does whatever he pleases and does so without acting on the grounds of obligations to anything or anyone other than himself. The salvation of the elect is included, and the Scriptures make this clear.

Even so, the same Scriptures likewise make clear that he pleases to save *believers*, and this is the key to our understanding. Again, I do not wish to repeat things, in detail, that I have dealt with elsewhere, but I think this chapter calls for a response to some of the passages that Luther or Calvin or Edwards would have used, and did use, to contend that God's salvation of some, by his sovereign providence, rules out free will.

The Case of Pharaoh

I begin with the matter of the hardening of Pharaoh's heart as described in Exodus, starting in 4:21. This is something of a test case in the Arminian-Calvinist debate, not only because Calvinists make use of it but, more important, because Paul himself uses the case of Pharaoh in Romans 9.

It matters little whether the *first* reference, in Exodus, is to God's hardening Pharaoh's heart or to Pharaoh's doing so; both statements occur in the section. Indeed, this first one is God's statement, "I will harden his heart, so that he will not let the people go." Subsequently the record states that Pharaoh hardened his heart (as in 8:15), but it also reports that God hardened Pharaoh's heart (as in 9:12).

What does this tell us about the sovereignty and providence of God, either in general or in matters of salvation? At least in general, it tells us that God is governing all things toward his desired ends, including Pharaoh's heart and refusal to let Israel go from Egypt. But a modicum of care with the passage and its implications will keep us from seeing there the idea that it argues against free will in responding to or rejecting God's gracious offer of salvation in Jesus Christ. More than one factor is involved, all of them requiring careful biblical exposition.

First is the fact that God hardened Pharaoh's heart *so that he would not let the people go*, as 4:21 and the entire story confirm. This is not the same thing as personal salvation. Perhaps Proverbs 21:1 should be mentioned here again: "The king's heart is in the hand of the Lord. Like the rivers of water, He turns it wherever He wishes." It is highly unlikely, given the nature of Proverbs, that this refers to personal salvation. There is no reason to resist the idea that, at various junctures of history, God "turns" the heart or will of persons to make decisions that are in accord with his providential purpose. I know of no one who would dispute that.

Second is the fact that when God acts in such a way as this, he does not necessarily reach within a person's heart or mind and "flip a switch" that registers a decision by the person involved. God knows human hearts perfectly, and he knows how individuals will respond to various stimuli. So when he told Moses he would harden Pharaoh's heart, the best way to understand that is that *he would do what he knew Pharaoh would reject*. That way, he could bring about the hardening of Pharaoh's heart without in the least interfering with Pharaoh's free will or directly hardening it himself.

For that matter, and third, Pharaoh's might well have been a "special case." Even if God overrode Pharaoh's natural inclination (and there is no reason to suspect this), we could not object. There are cases, in Scripture, where persons have reached a point of no return in God's dealings with them, so that he writes them off, so to speak, and acts in a way that he knows will serve to confirm their rejection of him. Such acts are, essentially, *judgments*. Romans 1 speaks of those whom God in judgment "gave up" or "gave over" (vv. 24, 26, 28). In 2 Thessalonians 2:9–11 Paul speaks of those to whom God sends "strong delusion, that they should believe the lie" because they had already rejected the truth. I strongly suspect that this was the case with Pharaoh: God judicially acted in a way that he knew would harden his heart.

Romans 9:14–24

This brings us, then, to Romans 9:14–24, a passage that is cited whenever someone defends the sovereignty of God in applying salvation only to those whom he unconditionally chose before he created the world. As I have already indicated, there is no question that God "has mercy on whom He wills, and whom He wills He hardens" (v. 18), or that as the divine "potter" he makes both the vessels in whom he will demonstrate his mercy and the ones in whom he will demonstrate his holy wrath (vv. 21–23). This is, ultimately, no different from what has already been quoted from Psalm 115:3: "Our God is in heaven; He does whatever He pleases." The sovereign God in his all-encompassing providence governs the world in accord with his infallible purpose.

That God saves whom he pleases, and does whatever he pleases, however, does not tell us how he pleases to do these things or, more important, whom he pleases to save. Yet we do not need to relegate this to his secret will, to the things he has chosen not to reveal to us. For he has revealed this: he pleases to save *believers*.[2] First Corinthians 1:21 makes this clear, referring (I have no doubt) to the eternal good pleasure of God: "In the wisdom of God . . . it pleased God through the foolishness of the message preached to save those who believe." John 6:40 says the same thing: "This is the will of Him who sent Me, that everyone who sees the Son and believes in Him may have everlasting life."[3]

In the discussion of Romans 9, it is even more important to recognize that Paul does not leave us uncertain about this. Yes, God saves whom he pleases, and in his pleasure he has rejected some of the Israelites who might otherwise have thought themselves elected to his saving grace. But those Israelites are not rejected for no other reason than that the Almighty Potter made them for that destiny. Instead, they are rejected for this specific reason: "Because they did not seek it [righteousness before God] by faith, but as it were by the works of the law" (v. 32). In 10:3 Paul repeats: "They being ignorant of God's righteousness, and seeking to establish their own righteousness, have not submitted to the righteousness of God." And in 11:20 he says it again: "Because of unbelief they were broken off."

---

2. I use "believers" in the fullest, pregnant sense of the word as it is used for genuine, saving faith and all that is implied by that. It is beyond my purpose, here, to expand on this.

3. I avoid, here, the inclination to expand on this at length and refer the reader to my *Grace, Faith, Free Will*.

To be sure, then, the matter of deciding whom to save rests squarely within the sovereignty of a God who governs the world according to his own plan. In that sovereignty he has freely and without obligation chosen to save those who exercise faith in the provision he has made in Jesus Christ. All of Romans 9–11 makes good sense in this framework.

Acts 13:48

I take space, here, for just one more passage, likewise made use of by those who argue that the sovereign administration of grace rules out the free exercise of the human will. This passage is in Acts 13, which describes the ministry of Paul and Barnabas in Pisidian Antioch on the first missionary journey. The key words seized on by the advocates of God's ordaining of all things are in verse 48: "As many as had been appointed to eternal life believed." The Authorized Version reads, "As many as were ordained to eternal life." Perhaps the word *ordained* contributes to the tendency to cite the verse in the discussion of the role of free will, since it is easy to assume that what God ordains cannot be by free will. There are two important things to be said about the implications of this statement.

First, as is always true in interpreting the Scripture, the context is important. And the context has another statement that in effect clarifies the meaning of this one. That is in verse 46, where Paul is quoted as saying to the larger group, which included disbelieving Jews, "It was necessary that the word of God should be spoken to you first; but since you reject it, *and judge yourselves unworthy of everlasting life*, behold, we turn to the Gentiles." Immediately, then, we read that as many of the Gentiles "as were ordained/ appointed to eternal life" put faith (in Jesus). In other words, those who "were ordained" to eternal life were those who did *not* "judge themselves unworthy" of eternal life.

Second, this becomes even more understandable when we examine the verb "were ordained/appointed." The form is a participle of the Greek *tetagmai*, which can be middle or passive voice. The verb itself (*tassō*) means basically to put in place or place in position and can have a broad range of meanings that grow out of that. It seems reasonably clear to me that the form here is either in the middle voice or is a passive used like a middle and without any suggestion of another agent. The parallel with "judge yourselves unworthy of eternal life" strengthens this understanding. In that light, then, the verb means that these Gentiles who had put themselves in position for eternal life (in contrast to the Jews who judged themselves unworthy of eternal life) put their faith in Jesus as their Savior.

Even in the English language a passive voice verb can be used with such a "middle" sense, having no reference at all to some agent other than oneself. Thus we say, for example, "I am disposed" to do something or other, or "I am inclined" to act in a certain way, and we do not mean that someone else has disposed or inclined us. Even the English verb that matches the one used here in Acts 13:48 can be used that way: "I was positioned for action" simply means that I put myself in the position needed for action. Furthermore, the verb used here is not the one typically used (Greek *orizō*) for God's ordaining of things.

There is no convincing reason, then, to think that Acts 13:48 means that God had already ordained or appointed to eternal life those who were saved by faith in Antioch. There is, of course, an eternal election of believers by God, but it is not the pattern of the New Testament to speak of that as the grounds for their salvation.

Conclusion

When one stops to think carefully about God's sovereignty, there is no reason to consider that in some way it stands in contradiction to human freedom of will as described in Scripture and defined in this volume. Of course, if that freedom meant that humanity could overthrow God's government or act against what God determined to allow, that would be impossible. But free will does not mean that.

I am not suggesting that we can fully explain every aspect of how God's sovereign government of the universe and human free will work together. But I am suggesting that the two truths do not need "reconciling." The understanding of them requires, at root, just this simple observation: if God sovereignly ordained that humans have free will, then their exercise of it in no way encroaches on his sovereignty. And we are assured that humans could have no will of any kind, free or otherwise, if God did not sovereignly create them so.

Nor is there any contradiction between God's all-encompassing government and human free will. No one that I know questions that God rules absolutely over all that transpires in the world, including humans' free choices, and incorporates all of that into his plan.

It would seem, in fact, that the idea of free will actually serves to *en-hance* or *magnify* the sovereign government of God. It would be one thing for God to create and bring to his desired ends the actions and destinies of automatons who could do only as they were programmed. Our God is far more capable—omnipotent—than that: he can set people free to choose to serve him or reject him and still accomplish all his purposes in the world.

10

Free Will and the Logic of Cause and Effect

THE PURPOSE OF THIS chapter is to respond, directly, to the rationalism of Jonathan Edwards against free will. In particular, I refer to the logical arguments he set forth that are dependent on his use of cause-and-effect relationships, an approach that neither Luther nor Calvin took. Edwards also argued against free will on the basis of foreknowledge and necessity, and my earlier chapter on that topic was intended to respond both to him and to Luther. Here, then, I confine myself to his logical objections.

I refer the reader to the earlier chapter on Edwards and free will. There is no need to repeat, here, the summary of his presentation that I have given there. Even so, I will review that presentation, focus on its key elements, and respond. All the while, I feel a little uncomfortable, in that rationalism is not the way to do theology. Still, I am aware that many people find Edwards's approach impressive, and so I do not ignore his argument entirely.

For the purposes of my response, then, I observe (1) that Edwards everywhere assumes the universal applicability of cause-effect relationships to everything that transpires in the universe; and (2) that, on this grounds, he regards the concept of self-determinism as absurd. I will deal with these two major aspects of his approach in reverse order.

Edwards against Self-Determinism

I have described Edwards's impatience with self-determinism in the earlier chapter on him. Apparently growing out of his commitment to universal cause-effect relationships, he felt compelled to hold up for ridicule the idea of self-determinism, insisting that this Arminian notion requires that human volition be both an effect and its cause and thus two logically distinguishable "events." This lies under one of his most basic arguments against the Arminian understanding of freedom of the will as he interprets the Arminian view.

I include, here, a lengthy quotation from Edwards on this point, being the analysis that follows his assertion that the Arminian notion of liberty means that there is a "sovereignty in the will, whereby it has power to determine its own volitions."

> If the will determines itself, then either the will is active in determining its volitions, or it is not. If it be active in it, then the determination is an *act* of the will; and so there is one act of the will determining another. But if the will is not active in the determination, then how does it exercise any liberty in it? These gentlemen [advocates for free will] suppose that the thing wherein the will exercises liberty, is in its determining its own acts. But how can this be, if it ben't active in determining? Certainly the will, or the soul, can't exercise any liberty in that wherein it don't act, or wherein it don't exercise itself. So that if either part of this dilemma be taken, this scheme of liberty, consisting in self-determining power, is overthrown. If there be an act of the will in determining all its own free acts, then one free act of the will is determined by another; and so we have the absurdity of every free act, even the very first, determined by a foregoing free act. But if there be no act or exercise of the will in determining its own acts, then no liberty is exercised in determining them. From whence it follows, that no liberty consists in the will's power to determine its own acts: or, which is the same thing, that there is no such thing as liberty consisting in a self-determining power of the will. (*FW* 176)

More than one thing needs to be said about this paragraph from Edwards, the first being that it is an excellent example of what is often elaborate, not to say torturous, reasoning, followed only with considerable difficulty. Oliver Wendell Holmes is reported to have said of *Freedom of the Will* that it is like "the unleavened bread of the Israelite: holy it may be, but heavy it actually is."[1]

A more important observation is that the paragraph illustrates well Edwards's rationalistic method, first by analysis framing the argument in two exclusive and exhaustive possibilities: if the will determines itself, it is either active in doing so or not. From that comes the argument that if it *is* active, there must be one act of the will preceding and determining the

---

1. Sweeney, *Jonathan Edwards and the Ministry of the Word*, 148.

other; and if it is *not* active, it is not exercising liberty at all. Then follows the conclusion that, either way, the idea that humans are at liberty to exercise self-determining power is self-defeating.

Edwards's argument, here, depends entirely on the analysis of the proposition that Arminian freedom of the will means a power to determine one's own volitions. That analysis reveals, for Edwards, that in the Arminian notion of liberty there are two events, as indicated by the two words: namely, the *determining* (as the cause) and then the *volition* that follows from it (as the effect). It is this analysis that sets up his logical argument.

What Edwards is doing is defining *self-determination* to mean that the will must choose its own actions in order to determine them. This means that there is an act of the will that determines any given act of the will, a choice preceding a choice, as it were. But if all human choices are self-determined, then the choice preceding the choice must likewise have a choice or volition that precedes that. And this will lead us to infinite regress, with every choice requiring a preceding choice and no place to stop, going back into the infinite past. The possible logical solutions to this are two. (1) Stop with some choice, back there, that was *not* "caused" by a prior choice and so was uncaused. This is not possible, since anything uncaused must either exist eternally or cannot exist. (2) Stop with a choice, back there, that was caused by some agent outside the self. But that would make the first choice *not* self-determined or "free," which would then mean that the resulting volitions in the whole chain of cause-effect relationships would also not be self-determined.

There are two things wrong with this. First and most important is finding in the power of self-determination two events instead of one. One simply does not first will to make a choice or volition and then exercise his will in choosing. A person does not choose to choose; he simply chooses— regardless what influences are involved and exist prior to the choice. In other words, no one who holds to self-determinism means by it what Edwards (deliberately, I assume) took it to mean.

For that matter, Edwards himself appears to realize that this is not what those who defend free will mean. In one discussion he acknowledges that the Arminian really means that "the person in the exercise of a power of willing and choosing, or the soul acting voluntarily, determines [a course of action]" (*FW* 172)—thus undermining his analysis as so much quibbling over words.

Even so, it would be impossible to overstate the importance of this argument for Edwards's entire volume. Again and again he returns to the very same analysis and weaves it into his argument (*FW* 192, 219–20, 228–29,

234–35, 359, etc.). He was apparently convinced that the Arminian logically *had* to mean what he took self-determinism to mean rather than what the Arminian *really* meant.

The second thing wrong with Edwards's analysis is this: even if it were true that there were two free acts in a given volition, Edwards was wrong to indicate (partly by implication here, but by direct statement in other places) that this required the impossible infinite regress. My reason for saying this is, I think, fairly obvious. Any Christian, including the one who believes in self-determination, traces the beginning of persons back, not to infinite regress, but to a self-existent Creator God. God created *persons*, and persons are the selves that make choices or—as Edwards himself put it, cited above—voluntarily determine a course of action. Edwards obfuscated this by saying that the Arminians said that the *will* has power to determine its volitions. Defenders of free will either don't say that or, if they do, say it carelessly. They say, instead, that *persons* determine their volitions. *Self*-determination means that the *self* or *person* wills, and in that volition chooses or determines or decides on a course of action.

I cite the editors of a recent edition of some of Edwards's works, commenting on his insistence that freedom is "the 'liberty' or opportunity to do as one pleases in the absence of any hindrance":

> Edwards is, of course, assuming that this is the meaning of liberty in "common speech," and he takes advantage at this point of the ambiguity previously noted about whether the issue is the freedom of the *person* or the freedom of the *will* to insist on the former, declaring that liberty belongs to the person and not to the will. Accordingly, he can claim that the notion of a self-determining *will* is incoherent because it is supposed to be independent of any prior conditions, and this leads to an infinite regress: before any free act, there must be another free act and so on, and in order to stop the regress, there must be a first act that is not free. But if this is so, no subsequent act can be free. Here we have the basic contention of the entire treatise, and for Edwards it was enough to overcome the Arminian position.[2]

I cannot imagine that *anyone*—Arminian or otherwise—would ever have thought that freedom of the will means anything other than freedom of the *person* to exercise his or her will.

---

2. Smith, Stout, Minkema, *Jonathan Edwards Reader*, xvi.

As a final observation on this point, I note that Calvin himself approvingly used the term *self-determination* to refer to humans' exercise of the will, in his discussion of the difference between coercion and necessity. A coerced will, he said, would be one "forcibly driven by an external impulse." By contrast, a will is self-determined when "it directs itself in the direction in which it is led, when it is not taken by force or dragged unwillingly." That a human will is self-determined, he continued to say, means that "if he does anything evil, it should be imputed to . . . his own voluntary choosing." Yes, humans sin by necessity, but this is located "precisely in corruption of the will, from which it follows that it is self-determined" (*BLW* 69–70). Again: "We hold that the will can be called free only because it moves by a self-determined volition" (*BLW* 122). Subsequently he cites Augustine in agreement on this terminology (*BLW* 140–41).

For Calvin, then, the problem with free will lies not in some logical absurdity in the term *self-determination* but in the very real effects of depravity, which is an entirely different matter, one that I have dealt with in an earlier chapter.

Edwards and the Logic of Cause and Effect

For Edwards, free will fails because it leaves human choices without causes. Again, I refer the reader to the earlier chapter on Edwards for other observations about his method and approach. Without repeating much of what is said there, I note that fundamental to all of Edwards's arguments is the basic assumption that the law of cause and effect applies to everything that occurs in the universe, including specifically the choices that persons make.

I think Edwards himself would acknowledge that if this foundational assumption were undermined, his argument against free will as a whole would crumble. He makes no bones about its importance for his position. He regards this as "the first dictate of the common and natural sense which God hath implanted in the minds of all mankind," and then says, "If this grand principle of common sense be taken away, all arguing from effects to causes ceaseth, and so all knowledge of any existence. . . . Particularly all our proof of the being of God ceases" (*FW* 181).

What does Edwards mean by *cause*? He observes that the word is often used narrowly to refer only to "that which has a positive efficiency or influence to produce a thing, or bring it to pass." But he will use it "in a sense which is more extensive," he says: "to signify any antecedent . . . on which an event, either a thing, or the manner and circumstance of a thing, so depends, that it is the ground and reason, either in whole, or in part, why it is, rather than not; or why it is as it is, rather than otherwise." "In other words," he says, a *cause* is "any antecedent with which a consequent event is so connected, that it truly belongs to the reason why the proposition which affirms that event, is true; *whether it has any positive influence, or not*" (FW 180–81, italics mine).

I will make two relatively brief comments. First is the fact that Edwards is indeed giving *cause* a meaning that is broader than the one usually given to it. Later in the same section he makes it broad enough to include the "occasion" for an event. As becomes clear in his subsequent discussion of the fact that God is not the author of sin, this allows him to include God's permissive decree about sin as *cause*. Thus any antecedent event that has a necessary connection to an event is its cause. This is not the way the word is typically used in theological discussion.

More important is the fact that Edwards is applying the same cause-effect law that governs actions in the physical world to actions in the psyche. And that is questionable indeed. Even on his broad definition of *cause*, he ought not use the language of cause and effect to define human volition. In the material world this language indicates mechanical connections that cannot be otherwise than they are and are as regular as clockwork. Edwards says that "if every act of the will is excited by a motive, then that motive is the cause of the act of the will," that motives do what they do "by their influence; and so much as is done by their influence, is the effect of them" (FW 225).[3] No. An influence is not properly named a cause; an influence can be resisted.

It is true, of course, that promptings arising in the psyche can themselves cause motions (actions) in the physical world. As I write this, my inner decisions to give existence to printed words on a page, via my computer's word processing program, are translated into mechanical events that include the motions of my fingers, the pressing of keys on the keyboard, and the electronic conversion of those motions into words visible on the screen and stored in the computer's memory. But is it correct to say that my decisions are *caused* by other things—whatever mental "things" they might be—that bear the same relationship to my volitions that pressing keys on my keyboard does to the words on my computer screen? I pull the trigger

---

3. Guelzo, "Jonathan Edwards and the Possibilities of Free Will," 92. He reads Edwards to say, furthermore, that "the presentation of these motives in all future moments has already been fixed." I assume Edwards thought so, but his argument in *Freedom of the Will* does not contend for this: *certain*, yes, but not *fixed*. See the chapter on foreknowledge and necessity.

on a gun and kill someone. All the physical actions are purely mechanical, manifesting inviolable cause-effect laws. But is my decision to kill likewise mechanical, manifesting inviolable cause-effect laws?

I think not. I think, instead, that decisions of the will are not the inevitable effects of prior causes—and, furthermore, if they are then, like all the manifestations of natural law, they go back either into infinite regress or to an uncaused Cause of everything who becomes responsible for it all. But the mental world does not function like the physical world. Decisions of the will do not spring up without antecedents, of course; they come about as a result of ideas, persuasions, influences, and the like. Even so, influence and response provide a much better framework for the discussion of the mind and its functions, including the will, than cause and effect.

To go back to Edwards's analysis of his opponents' view of free will into two acts, I would simply observe that the only reality, other than contingent circumstances, antecedent to a volition is the *self*. Edwards himself is much better on this point when he defines *will* as a "faculty or power or principle of mind by which it is capable of choosing: an act of the will is the same as an act of choosing or choice" (*FW* 137).

I acknowledge that there are questions that result from the kind of dualism I am affirming. If our minds and wills are not part of the material world and do not function like the material world, there is a genuine difficulty in understanding how a mental prompting can in fact *cause* a physical motion. This is the classic problem of philosophy called "the mind-body problem." If the psyche is a sort of "stuff" that is entirely different from the "stuff" of my physical body, how can they interact?

René Descartes speculated that there is some sort of "connection" between them in the pineal gland. That "solution" is no solution at all, as also are a number of solutions proposed by philosophers. Some claim that the physical world is, after all, part of the mind. Some take the opposite approach and say that the so-called mind is nothing more than a physical brain with electric currents. That "solution" leads, of course, to philosophical materialism or naturalism, which affirms that everything that exists is matter. In a materialistic world, it works very well to affirm that all events are effects of prior causes. I find it infinitely too hard to believe that this works in a biblical view of God, humanity, and things.

In other words, one of the powers of the human psyche is to "originate" ideas and to translate those ideas into actions that extend into the physical world. Our volitions are included among these. This does not mean, of course, that we operate in a vacuum. We live in and are influenced by the world about us and by others. From the moment we are born we have experiences, and those experiences contribute to who we are and how we think. We are affected by all the things that have influenced us at any given time.

This means that at times our free choices will be very predictable. But it does not mean that all our choices are necessary or fixed. In my treatment of compatibilism (or soft determinism) earlier, I have tried to show that regardless of the strength of our motivations, when we have the information and influence that enables us, we are free to choose between alternatives, to make more than one choice. That is, in fact, a given in human experience.

In short, Edwards was a compatibilist, one who claims that determinism and free will are compatible. But the "free will" that is compatible with determinism is not free. Instead it is bound in a world where just one choice is possible, a choice that is the infallible effect of a complex of causes that make it necessary.

Once deny that the minds of persons are part of the cause-effect system that prevails in the natural realm, however, and the argument of Edwards loses its power. His necessity is abrogated and the *person* is free to will. We can, at least, go back to the primary considerations that have always governed the issue of free will: foreknowledge and necessity, sovereignty and providence, and depravity and grace.

Part Four

In Conclusion

11

Summing Up, and the Bottom Line

The Case against Free Will

THE CASE THAT LUTHER, Calvin, and Edwards made against free will depends, finally, on the theology of the Calvinistic wing of the Reformation. Technically speaking, Luther was not a "Calvinist" and represents, instead, the Lutheran wing. But his reasons for rejecting free will were, at root, similar to those of Calvin. Edwards, as we have seen, mounted a rationalistic, rather than a theological, campaign against free will. But his final chapter, though not presented as part of his argument, reveals that the theological assumptions he sought to sustain by his rationalism were clearly Calvinistic.

The views offered by our three principals against free will, therefore, were primarily the following.

1. God's sovereign government of the world he created, including humankind, is of such a nature that everything transpires because he willed it to be part of his all-encompassing plan for things. From eternity he devised his plan and made his decisions (decrees) as to what would be. Those decisions control all events, including the choices or decisions made by human beings, and this control is of such a nature that when people act God is acting in and with them in such a way that they are "free" only to make the choices they make and which God wills for them to make.

2. God's exhaustive foreknowledge of the future, from before the foundation of the world, is of such a nature that only the course of events he foresees can transpire. Even if this foreknowledge did not logically rule out the possibility of choosing more than one course of action, the fact that God's foreknowledge is dependent on his foreordination of all things finally rules out such a possibility.

3. Free will, then, does not include the power of alternative choice, of making a choice that is different from the one a person makes. Even so, a person's will can be described as "free" so long as he or she chooses in accord with his or her nature. The choices of the unregenerate, then, are inevitably wicked, and the choices of the regenerate are inevitably good. Redemption, therefore, begins with the regenerating change of the person's nature, administered unconditionally by God on those whom he has chosen, for reasons known only to himself and for whom alone he has provided a means for their deliverance.

4. Indeed, then, human depravity makes it both logically and practically impossible for persons to exercise free will. Before regeneration, they can act only in accord with their depravity and that means they must always resist God and cannot turn to him or even prepare their hearts for the reception of God's favor.

5. Such unconditional favor exercised on behalf of those God has chosen (the elect) is grace. Salvation by grace requires that the work must be exclusively and wholly God's work, and that the human subject—object, actually—plays no part in receiving that grace. This, too, eliminates free will. Persons have no choice in whether to be saved, or else they would by that choice make a contribution to their salvation, and that would dilute grace.

In Defense of Free Will

I have attempted, in this volume, to set free will in a position that makes it entirely defensible in the context of the objections of Luther, Calvin, and Edwards. The previous chapters have provided the details, which I give here in summary.

1. The sovereignty of God is just as strong, if not stronger, in a world where human beings have the power of choice between alternatives. One reason for saying this is that God is the one who freely—sovereignly—decided to give this power to those he created to bear his image. Another is the fact that God is marvelously able to govern the world, and achieve his ends—for every individual and the world and human race as a whole—in spite of the fact that the persons he made exercise the freedom to choose (Psalm 135:6).

Nothing about this contradicts or conditions the sovereignty of God unless one interprets sovereignty to mean that God must be the only one who acts. But the Bible presents human beings as actors, too, and so when a person chooses for or against God he is fulfilling God's will that he have the choice—even if he violates God's will or desire that none perish (2 Peter 3:9). Furthermore, the choices of every person have been fully incorporated into the all-encompassing plan of God so that he providentially works all things for his own ends, which include the good of those whom he has lovingly identified as his own in response to their faith (Romans 8:28).

2. Human depravity is such that no person ever would respond to the gospel apart from a work of grace initiated by God. No person seeks God, so God must be the seeker. He has broken into history and provided his Son as atonement for our sins (1 John 2:2). Furthermore, he has announced the good news of salvation and packaged it in the *Word* of the gospel, by which he speaks to fallen humankind and invites them to come to him. Complementing that preached Word, he has sent the Spirit of his grace to convince the world of lost hearers that they are lost and condemned and that there is a way in Christ for them to be accounted righteous before God. By that "prevenient," wooing, convicting grace they are enabled to choose Christ, to put faith in him (Romans 10:13–14).

3. Nor is the grace of God diminished or diluted in any way as a result of the fact that the person is saved "by" faith. Indeed, the Bible insists that salvation is by faith for the very purpose that it may be by grace (Romans 4:16). So the work of salvation is wholly and exclusively God's. A person's accepting the gift contributes nothing to the work and subtracts nothing from the giver. The hands that people hold out to receive the gift are empty hands, offering no price or merit. Salvation is from beginning to end the work of God, and he alone receives the credit.

4. Furthermore, God's exhaustive foreknowledge of the future offers no contradiction of free will. Rightly understand, foreknowledge is knowledge in advance, not foreordination. To be sure, what God foreknows is certain, but he foreknows it because it is certain, not vice versa. That the future is certain is nothing more than that it is future, and it includes both all contingencies (which include alternatives that will be determined by human choice) and all necessities (which must be the way they will be, either as a result of natural law or of the decision of God to make them so regardless what humans would choose).

5. Nor do the laws of cause and effect contradict free will. In this universe there are both material or physical essences (bodies) and mental essences (minds), and they function differently in at least some ways. The physical world functions by mechanical, cause-effect laws. The mental world does not, and the exercise of the will lies within this realm. Minds

and wills are aspects of *persons*, and persons originate thoughts and volitions. This is not to say that they are without antecedents or they spring up, as it were, in a vacuum. There are antecedent states of mind and influences. But a person is able to make a decision, a choice, freely, one that is not made *necessary* as a result of those influences. This requires a measure of understanding, of course, at least enough that the person recognizes what the choices are. In the matter of responding to the gospel, the person who chooses for Christ will have experienced the understanding produced by the Word of God, made convincing by the Spirit of God.

The Bottom Line

In studying and interacting with Luther, Calvin, and Edwards I have asked myself, again, just what is the most basic difference between the Arminian wing and the Calvinistic wing of Reformed theology.

The difference is not the sovereignty and providence of God. Both sides agree that God is the sovereign Lord of the universe, that he is the one whose plan is being worked out in it all, that he governs in such a way that everything is incorporated into his plan, that he is in control. He and he alone determines who will be saved. If there is a condition for a person to meet, it is a condition that God freely established and did so only because he willed that it be that way.

The difference is not that salvation is by grace. Both sides agree that God alone does the saving. I know of no Christian, from among the laity in the pew or the theology professors in the seminary, who thinks he or she contributed anything at all to being saved. All alike will confess that salvation is initiated by God, that it is altogether by grace, and that even their faith is enabled by grace.

The difference is not the exhaustive foreknowledge of God. Although open theism muddied the waters some on this point, both sides agree that God knows the future perfectly and that everything in the future is certain to be what it will be. They may differ as to whether this foreknowledge is the result of foreordination, but they do not differ on the foreknowledge itself. And the difference in their view of foreordination grows out of the more basic difference.

The "bottom-line" difference is this. Calvin expressed it when he said that God judged "that the praise of his goodness and mercy shines better if he exhibits the proof of it only in some, while in others he displays an example of his wrath and judgment" (*BLW* 200). In other words, what lies at the root of the view of salvation held by Calvin (and those who have followed him) is this: As a result of the fall, the whole mass of humanity was lost, under the condemnation of God, depraved, living in wicked rebellion against God, unwilling—and unable to be willing—to turn to him. Out of that mass of humanity, God determined to save some and chose those whom he would save—and in whom he would do the whole work of saving them, and them only, without any conditions for them to meet. The rest of humanity he gave no opportunity to be saved and made no provision for.

That is stark, but it is Calvinism. And it is the reason free will is denied since in that picture there is no role for free will.

Over against that view of salvation is the view offered by classic, evangelical, Reformation Arminians. Start with the same first sentence above, describing the condition of the whole mass of humanity after the fall; that much is the same. Then, for all those in that mass of humanity God chose to make a provision for their salvation. He determined, further, to send forth those who would proclaim that provision and to shed abroad his Spirit to convince them of their predicament and his provision and so to enable them to accept that provision by faith or to reject it. Concomitantly, he determined to save those who would believe.

This is Reformation Arminianism, and it is the reason free will is affirmed since in that picture there is a role for free will.

The choice between these does not depend on which is more appealing to our natural minds or which strikes us as fairer. The Calvinist believes God is fair because all deserve eternal punishment. The choice between these—and here free will is also involved!—lies in which view fits the whole of Scripture better. That I have dealt with in the earlier chapter on free will in biblical perspective. (I have also dealt with it in full detail in my *Grace, Faith, Free Will* and need not attempt to repeat that material here.)

I will offer, however, that even if nothing else were involved, the Arminian view fits best with the biblical teachings that Christ died for all to make universal provision, that we are commanded to preach the gospel to all and so to hold out to all the offer of salvation, and that salvation—salvation as a whole, not merely justification—is *by faith*.

I think it obvious that Calvinism's salvation is not *by* faith but *to* faith. In that system of thought regeneration logically (if not chronologically) precedes faith. It must do so, since the depraved sinner is not capable of faith until God changes him or her from the inside out. Salvation by faith is conditional salvation; Calvinism's salvation is unconditional.

The Bible, however, is clear that salvation is by faith. That God's eternal will or good pleasure is to save believers. That he calls on people everywhere to repent and believe the gospel. And that in his infinite goodness and grace he makes it possible for fallen persons to choose to receive Christ by faith—and so to exercise free will.

Bibliography

Calvin, John. *The Bondage and Liberation of the Will: A Defence of the Orthodox Doctrine of Human Choice against Pighius.* Edited by A. N. S. Lane, translated by G. I. Davies. Grand Rapids: Baker, 1996.

Clouse, R. G. "Erasmus, Desiderius." In *Evangelical Dictionary of Theology*, edited by Walter A. Elwell. Grand Rapids: Baker, 1984.

Edwards, Jonathan. *Freedom of the Will.* Edited by Paul Ramsey. The Works of Jonathan Edwards 1. New Haven, CT: Yale University Press, 1957.

Geisler, Norman. *Christian Apologetics.* Grand Rapids: Baker, 1976.

———. "Freedom, Free Will, and Determinism." In *Evangelical Dictionary of Theology*, edited by Walter A. Elwell. Grand Rapids: Baker, 1984.

Guelzo, Allen C. "The Return of the Will: Jonathan Edwards and the Possibilities of Free Will." In *Edwards in Our Time: Jonathan Edwards and the Shaping of American Religion*, edited by Sang Hyun Lee and Allen C. Guelzo, 87–110. Grand Rapids: Eerdmans, 1999.

Heinze, R. W. "Luther, Martin." In *Evangelical Dictionary of Theology*, edited by Walter A. Elwell. Grand Rapids: Baker, 1984.

James, William. "The Dilemma of Determinism." *Unitarian Review*, September 1884. Reprinted in *The Will to Believe, and Other Essays in Popular Philosophy.* New York: Longmans, Green, 1956.

Kant, Immanuel. *The Critique of Practical Reason.* Great Books of the Western World 42. Chicago: University of Chicago Press, 1952, originally published 1788.

Keil, C. F., and F. Delitzsch. *Old Testament Commentaries*, vol. 1: *Genesis to Judges 6:32.* Grand Rapids: Associated Publishers and Authors, Inc., 1970.

Luther, Martin. *Martin Luther on the Bondage of the Will: A New Translation of* De Servo Arbitrio *(1525), Martin Luther's Reply to Erasmus of Rotterdam.* Translated by J. I. Packer and O. R. Johnston. Westwood, NJ: Revell, 1957.

Noll, Mark A. "Edwards, Jonathan." In *Evangelical Dictionary of Theology*, edited by Walter A. Elwell. Grand Rapids: Baker, 1984.

Picirilli, Robert E. "An Arminian Response to John Sanders's *The God Who Risks: A Theology of Providence.*" *JETS* 44 (2001) 467–91.

———. "Foreknowledge, Freedom, and the Future." *JETS* 43 (2000) 259–71.

―――. *Grace, Faith, Free Will: Contrasting Views of Salvation: Calvinism and Arminianism.* Nashville: Randall House, 2002.

―――. "Toward a Non-Deterministic Theology of Divine Providence." *Journal of Baptist Theology and Ministry* (the online journal of New Orleans Baptist Theological Seminary) 11 (2014) 38–61.

Reid, W. S. "Calvin, John. In *Evangelical Dictionary of Theology*, edited by Walter A. Elwell. Grand Rapids: Baker, 1984.

Smith, John E., Harry S. Stout, and Kenneth P. Minkema, editors. *A Jonathan Edwards Reader.* New Haven, CT: Yale Nota Bene, 1995.

Sweeney, Douglas A. *Jonathan Edwards and the Ministry of the Word.* Downers Grove, IL: IVP Academic, 2009.

Webster's New World College Dictionary. 3rd ed. New York: Macmillan, 1996.

Scripture Index

Old Testament

Genesis

2:16–17	19, 20
4:6–7	24
4:7	41
6:3	40
6:5	40, 47, 90
8:21	40, 47, 90

Exodus

4:21	112, 113
8:15	113
9:12	113

Leviticus

26:3–39	24–25

Deuteronomy

8:3	97
11:26–28	26
11:26	28
27	27
30	21

30:1	28
30:11–20	26
30:11–14	22
30:12–14	28
30:15	28
30:19	39
30:29	27

Joshua

8	27
24:14–15	29

1 Samuel

23:1–13	87

Psalms

14	94
14:7	22
115:3	19, 106, 114
119:130	97
126:1	22
135:6	44, 130

Proverbs

16:1	40, 102
21:1	40, 102, 113

Isaiah

1:19	21
40:1–2	40
40:6–7	40
45:9–10	110
53:6	94
66:2	57

Jeremiah

4:1	22
10:23	40

15:19	21
17:9	94
21:8	29
25:5	22
35:15	22

Ezekiel

18:23	21, 22

Zechariah

1:3	21

Malachi

1:2–3	40, 103

New Testament

Matthew

4	30
4:4	97
6:24	32
10:32–33	30
19:16–22	30
23:37	31

Mark

10:17–27	30
11:20	32

Luke

10:8	32
13:39	32
18:18–27	30

John

1:5	40
1:10–13	40
1:12	32
3:1ff	40
3:16	33
3:18	40, 42
3:27	40, 40
3:31	40
3:36	40
4:14	33
5:24	97
5:40	32
6:40	114
6:44	41, 95, 98
8:23	41
14:6	41
15:5	40
16:8	98
17:17	97

Acts

2:21	33
4:4	97
10:44	97
13:46	33, 115
13:48	115, 116
16:14	98
17:30	33
28:24	33

Romans

1:18ff	40
1:24	113
1:26	113
1:28	113
3:9ff	40, 47
3:12	94
3:19ff	40
3:20	21, 22, 22, 39, 90
3:21–26	40
4:2–3	40
4:16	131
4:25	96
5:12	16
5:12–19	94
5:20	22
7:9	22
7:23	91
8:5	40
8:14	48, 103
8:28	110, 131
9–11	115
9	112, 114
9:11–13	40, 103
9:14–24	114
9:15–16	46
9:18	19
9:20ff	40
9:30–31	40, 47
9:32	114
10:3	114
10:5–9	22
10:6–8	28
10:10–17	96

10:13–14	131
10:20	40
11:20	114
15:19	98

1 Corinthians

1:21	114
2:4–5	98
2:9	39, 90
10:11	25
11:7	5

2 Corinthians

3:17	99

Galatians

3:24	23

Ephesians

1:13	97
5:26	97

Colossians

1:5–6	97

1 Thessalonians

1:4	98
4:15	96

2 Thessalonians

2:9–11	113